Community Schools

Community Schools

People and Places Transforming Education and Communities

Edited by JoAnne Ferrara
and Reuben Jacobson

ROWMAN & LITTLEFIELD
Lanham • Boulder • New York • London

Published by Rowman & Littlefield
An imprint of The Rowman & Littlefield Publishing Group, Inc.
4501 Forbes Boulevard, Suite 200, Lanham, Maryland 20706
www.rowman.com

6 Tinworth Street, London SE11 5AL, United Kingdom

British Library Cataloguing in Publication Information Available

Library of Congress Cataloging-in-Publication Data Available

ISBN 978-1-4758-3140-5 (cloth : alk. paper)
ISBN 978-1-4758-3141-2 (pbk. : alk. paper)
ISBN 978-1-4758-3142-9 (electronic)

♾™ The paper used in this publication meets the minimum requirements of American National Standard for Information Sciences—Permanence of Paper for Printed Library Materials, ANSI/NISO Z39.48-1992.

This book is dedicated to Marty Blank and Jane Quinn, two community school visionaries and pioneers that planted a seed 25 years ago for today's community schools to grow and flourish. Their leadership provided the context to transform schools, communities, and lives of students and families.

Contents

Foreword

Dr. Jeannie Oakes, Presidential Professor of Education Equity Emeritus, UCLA, and Senior Fellow in Residence, Learning Policy Institute[1]

Today, high-quality educational opportunities are increasingly beyond the reach of many low-income students and students of color. This is not a new phenomenon, but a continuing trend—some say "slide"—that remains anchored by traditional schooling structures, prevailing norms of equality and inequality, and, not least, politics. So, what's a nation, a city, a school district to do?

This engaging and important book provides wise counsel to educators, policy makers, and activists seeking to stop and reverse that slide and give children in neighborhoods of poverty and racial isolation a better chance to prepare for full and productive lives.

In many underserved neighborhoods, children's limited opportunities are compounded by out-of-school barriers to learning, including trauma induced by housing instability, inadequate health care, food insecurity, and more broadly, racial animus. All conspire to limit the life chances of these vulnerable children. Typical school "reforms" are likely to position (or blame) these challenges as exogenous, community-based factors rather than seeing the school and its community as a coherent ecology in which schools have a crucial, but not sole responsibility for teaching, learning, and social betterment.

This book addresses this interplay of within-school and out-of-school structural deficiencies and possibilities. Drs. JoAnne Ferrara and Reuben Jacobson draw on their own considerable expertise and on the experiences of teachers, youth, families, leaders of schools, districts, and agencies to support the efforts of those seeking to use community schools. Such schools, in all their variety, are a powerful response to parochial distinctions that separate the potential of communities from the potential of children.

Ferrara, Jacobson, and their colleagues illuminate how community schools become a comprehensive, place-based strategy that both supports high-quality teaching and learning and addresses out-of-school barriers to success. They provide firsthand accounts of how diverse actors, working together, build partnerships between the school and other local entities—higher education institutions, government health and social service agencies, community-based nonprofits, and faith-based organizations. These partnerships intentionally seek to provide opportunities and supports that are enjoyed by students in better resourced schools in which the schools' work is routinely (but often invisibly) supplemented by high-capacity communities and families.

Community schools integrate health and social supports for children and families; they offer expanded learning time and opportunities; and they engage families and communities meaningfully in the life of the school. The most comprehensive community schools today seek to be social centers where families come together to strengthen neighborhoods and civil society more generally, as well as educate students well. The people in these schools accomplish this with collaborative approaches to leadership and practice.

Is this complicated, multi-faceted, people-intensive response worth the considerable effort? To answer that question, I have been studying community schools with a team of researchers at the Learning Policy Institute and the National Education Policy Center at the University of Colorado, Boulder—organizations both committed to conduct and communicate high-quality research to inform education policy decisions. Our goal was to review the research about community schools to determine whether the high hopes of advocates are supported by the evidence.

After reviewing more than 140 well-designed studies and comprehensive research reviews, the soundness of the community schools approach is unmistakable. Our report, "Community Schools as an Effective School Improvement Strategy," presents evidence that community schools meet the needs of low-achieving students in high-poverty schools and to help close opportunity and achievement gaps for students from low-income families, students of color, English learners, and students with disabilities. The four key pillars of community schools—integrated student services, expanded learning time and opportunities, meaningful parent and community engagement, and collaborative leadership and practice—promote conditions and practices found in high-quality schools and address out-of-school barriers to learning. Comprehensive community school interventions around the country show improvements in student outcomes, including attendance, academic achievement, high school graduation rates, and reduced racial and economic achievement gaps.[2]

The research base also offers clear lessons about how to achieve these outcomes. Strong implementation requires attention to all elements of the community schools model and to their placement at the center of the school. Community schools benefit from maintaining a strong academic improvement focus, and students benefit most from schools that offer more intense or sustained services. That being said, successful community schools do not all look alike. As described in this book, they leverage local assets and people to meet local needs, and they modify programming over time in response to changes in the school and community. They allow sufficient time for the strategy to fully mature.

Obviously, community schools alone cannot overcome all problems facing poor neighborhoods—that would require substantial investments in job training, housing and social safety net infrastructure, and other poverty alleviation measures. But what they can do is connect children and families to resources, opportunities, and supports that help offset the harms of poverty, foster healthy development, and promote learning. This book provides extraordinarily helpful accounts of how this good work can be done.

Acknowledgments

We would like to thank the contributors to this book first and foremost. We wanted to create a book about the educators, professionals, and family and community members working in community schools that was written by practitioners. We solicited contributors who are experienced and are working to improve the lives of children and families in our nation's most challenging schools and communities on a daily basis. The authors we selected saw the value in sharing their story so that others can learn what they do, how they do it, and what advice they have for the journey. We are grateful for the effort they made, their willingness to consider our feedback, and most significantly, their honesty about what has been successful, and what challenges remain, as they go about their important work.

The community schools field is full of supportive individuals who all believe in the power of collaboration and helping one another. Many people kept us motivated through the writing and editing process. They were enthusiastic about the purpose of this book and that gave us inspiration. Special thanks to the Coalition for Community Schools staff for the work they do to support the individuals filling these important roles through their commitment, leadership, resources, and networks.

Many people gave us feedback on the book. A special thank you to Marty Blank for his valuable perspective as a leader of the community schools field for over 20 years. Thank you, also, to Helen Jane Malone for her advice and encouragement.

Thanks to our families for supporting us. Especially to Reuben's wife, Mara Karlin and Reuben's parents, Jack and Bonnie Jacobson for their advice. JoAnne thanks her husband, Frank, for his ongoing support of her work.

Our publisher, Tom Koerner of Rowman & Littlefield, also deserves thanks for his interest and for seeing the value of a book about a growing education reform strategy. There is a lot yet to be written about community schools—our publisher has given us an opportunity to make a contribution to that literature. A special thanks to managing editor Carlie Wall for her patience and encouragement. We also are thankful for graduate assistant Carissa Burgard for editing skills and attention to details.

Collaborating on an edited volume was a new experience for each of us. We'd like to thank one another for commitment, patience, and belief in this endeavor.

Finally, thank you to all the leaders filling important roles in community schools from California to Florida and from Michigan to Texas. We know how hard you work. Your commitment to students and families brings us hope.

A heartfelt thank you to Jeannie Oakes for her decades of contributions to the education field and her willingness to write the foreword to this book.

Introduction

JoAnne Ferrara and Reuben Jacobson

It's early spring and Manny has been suspended from 2nd grade for throwing a desk at his teacher. Since kindergarten Manny has had many angry outbursts. Furthermore, he was asthmatic, separated from his parents, and diagnosed with behavioral and attention deficit disorders. At the time, he and his five siblings were being cared for by their ailing maternal grandmother. Both parents were incarcerated for drug-related crimes. The teacher and the assistant principal decided to walk the two blocks from the school to visit Manny at home. Upon entering the apartment, they became quite upset by Manny's living conditions and the lack of basic amenities available to him. Much to their surprise, they saw a kitchen with bowls of food on the floor and an unplugged refrigerator with its door hanging from the hinge. In the two rooms serving as bedrooms they saw six mattresses lying on the floor to accommodate Manny and his five siblings. Grandma told the principal and teacher that she often kept Manny's elder sister home from school to help care for their younger siblings. Grandma also shared that she was unable to get to the local clinic for Manny's asthma and ADD medication, or the wellness visits for his two-yea-old brother. After the 30-minute home visit they understood more about Manny's life than in the previous three years of his school experience. Of course he was traumatized; he was fighting for his life.

This real life account took place in a high poverty, drug-infested neighborhood in 1987. This school, like others at the time, lacked the resources to combat the overwhelming challenges of its students. As might be expected, a preponderance of schools suffered from systemic disadvantage, often struggling to provide a comprehensive network of support to meet students' needs.

Imagine the trajectory of Manny's life, and those of his siblings, if the year was 2019 and the collaborative team approach of the community school strategy was in place. Imagine, if after the home visit, community school partners convened a meeting to provide Manny and his family with access to the services they needed. The conversation around the table among the principal, community school coordinator, school-based health partner, the mental health practitioner, and the after-school coordinator would surely identify solutions to safeguard Manny from further obstacles to his well-being and learning. Certainly, if the collective team efforts of the community school partners had been available to this family, their story would have been less daunting.

As community schools become widely recognized as a strategy to strengthen outcomes for students and families in our most vulnerable neighborhoods, it is important that educators, family and community members, youth, nonprofits, institutions of higher education, the faith-based community, and others share an understanding of the roles individuals play in creating successful community schools. This book is intended to help readers discover their role and share in a new vision of how to operate all of our schools as a community school.

When the people in these roles, what many refer to as the community school's "stakeholders," work alongside one another they create an ethos of "pastoral care" for underserved students and their neighborhoods. Inherent in this equity philosophy is the belief that all children, regardless of their zip code, deserve access to those opportunities that foster success in life. With this in mind, educators and stakeholders begin a journey that shifts their notion of schooling from solely an academic enterprise, to a holistic approach focused on students' needs and community resources.

WHAT IS A COMMUNITY SCHOOL?

Community schools have a long history, are customizable to each city, district, and school site, and have many definitions. For more than 100 years community schools have been centers of their communities, have provided services and programs to students and families in need, and have been led collaboratively by education, family, and community leaders. Different models have emerged such as:

- Lead-partner model (pioneered by the Children's Aid in New York City),
- Beacons,
- Communities in Schools, and
- University-assisted (championed by the Netter Center for Community Partnerships at the University of Pennsylvania).

And there are many schools that operate as community schools but don't describe themselves that way. They are simply doing the work. However, we have learned a lot about community schools over the years. The Coalition for Community Schools, an alliance of partners across sectors and at all levels working to promote the strategy, uses the following definition:

> Using schools as hubs, community schools bring educators, families, and community partners together to offer a range of opportunities, supports, and services to children, youth as well as their families and communities. Community schools:
>
> - Provide expanded learning opportunities that are motivating and engaging during the school day, after school, and in the summer;
> - Offer essential health and social supports and services; and
> - Engage families and communities as assets in the lives of their children and youth.
>
> Every community school responds to unique local needs and includes the voices of students, families, and residents. Schools become centers of the community and are open to everyone—beyond school hours, including evenings and weekends. (Coalition for Community Schools, n.d.)

The National Center for Community Schools at Children's Aid describes a community school this way:

> Through extended hours, services and relationships, community schools reconceive education as a coordinated, child-centered effort in which schools, families and communities work together to support students' educational success, build stronger families and improve communities. (Lubell & Children's Aid Society, 2011)

And in their review of the research on community schools, the Learning Policy Institute and the National Education Policy Center identify four pillars or common features for all community schools, including:

1. Integrated student supports
2. Expanded learning time and opportunities
3. Family and community engagement
4. Collaborative leadership and practice (2017, p. 9).

Organizers fighting for "sustainable community schools" and the National Education Association describe six pillars of the community school strategy:

- Strong and proven curriculum
- High-quality teaching
- Inclusive leadership
- Positive behavior practices
- Family and community partnerships
- Community support services (National Education Association, 2017).

It isn't hard to see that many stakeholders have a perspective on what makes a community school. In addition to these various definitions, in 2017 the Coalition for Community Schools and its many partners developed standards that characterized the key elements of a community school. Under the standards' guiding principles, community schools:

- Pursue equity
- Invest in a whole-child approach to education
- Build on community strengths to ensure conditions for learning
- Use data and community wisdom to guide partnerships, programs, and progress
- Commit to interdependence and shared accountability
- Invest in building trusting relationships
- Foster a learning organization

The standards go on to describe two main parts of a community school, its structures and functions (e.g., coordinator position, collaborative leadership body, intentional and aligned planning) and its commonly implemented opportunities (e.g., powerful learning, integrated health and social supports, community engagement, and family engagement).[1] Whatever definition a school, district, or partner organization may use, community schools share common structural, functional, and programmatic features.

The purpose of this book is to describe the roles of collaborative leaders in the community school. To be clear, each role in a mature community school is a leadership role, from the principal to the student, from the community member to the after-school partner. While much has been written about the various characteristics of a community school including its programming, theory of action, and impact, far less has been written about the unique roles that make up a community school.

This book is different because it puts the people at the forefront of the community school story. The teacher, student, family member, principal, community school coordinator, and district leader all work together to create the governing bodies, processes, and programs required of a comprehensive and collaborative approach that meets the needs of each and every child.

We believe this book illuminates the uniqueness of each role, the ways in which different roles rely on one another, and where the work is mutually beneficial. We wanted to help the growing numbers of people interested in community schools have a better understanding of the roles they can play in an effective community school. The people working together in a community school are the focus of this book. If we believe in the idea of the African proverb that "it takes a village," then this is the book that answers, "who are the village people?"

Regardless of the role featured, common themes emerge across the chapters. *Kids matter* and are at the center of the work. *Place matters* and schools are uniquely situated to reach all students. *Partnerships matter* and are the unique element that brings individuals and institutions across a community together in joint cause. *Collaboration matters* because no one role and no single institution can address all the needs children and families from all backgrounds bring to school. While each of the following chapters features a particular role in a community school, the chapters are filled with examples of people working together toward a shared vision of thriving students.

HOW THIS BOOK IS ORGANIZED

Each contributor demonstrates the ways in which their work sets a context for groundbreaking community school initiatives. The partners and educators are leading the charge to change the lives of children, empower families, and revitalize communities. In doing so, these individuals use the power of collaboration to identify solutions, opportunities, and services to strengthen schools and communities. Simply put, the time has come to connect hearts and mind so that the Mannys of the world no longer merely survive, but thrive.

Both of us have worked in the community schools' field for over a decade. From our respective roles as teacher educator and policy maker we bring years of experience advocating for micro- and macro-level changes in schools. With this in mind, we invited authors to write chapters for this book because they had firsthand experience practicing or researching the different roles in a community school. Each chapter has the unique style and voice of its authors. We are grateful for their thoughtfulness and the effort they have given to sharing the role they feature with you.

In order to set the context for this work, we begin with Jacobson's review of the history of the community school movement, an analysis of the current state of the field, and possible future directions. We then move to the important roles that make up a community school.

In chapter 2 Tredway and Militello re-imagine what school leadership looks like in a community school. The chapter creates the context for leadership featuring two community school principals on their journey to re-imagine their roles and restructure the ways in which schools operate to provide equity and access for the constituents they serve.

Chapters 3 and 4 examine the roles of teachers and preservice teachers in community schools. Pais, Hurst, Rosenbaum, Lowe, and Wadle showcase their work at Humanitas Academy of Art and Technology (HAAT) community school in East Los Angeles. Through their community school experience the authors identify the types of supports and mind-set needed by teachers to create a high functioning teacher-led community school. Ferrara and Gómez discuss the preparation of preservice teachers in a community school with a glimpse at how novice teachers become a catalyst for deepening professional learning communities.

The critical role of the community school coordinator is the focus of chapter 5. While most readers will be familiar with the roles teachers and principals play in a school, the coordinator is a position unique to the community school approach. Gomez brings to life the behind the scenes strategies coordinators use to successfully manage a community school. Included in the discussion is a vignette from Community School Coordinator Liz Thacker about the county-wide initiative at Knoxville's Greater School Partnership.

In chapter 6, Hester and Capers underscore the key roles parents and community engagement play in both the design and transformation of schools. The authors offer practical strategies to engage families, as well as examples from their work with New York City's community school initiative.

The role of youth is often missing in community school literature. In acknowledging the obstacles to school engagement and success many minority youth face, chapter 7 authors Fehrer and Lopez take a fresh look at youth leadership in Oakland community schools. Their thoughtful discussion takes readers on a journey of school transformation inspired by youth activism and commitment.

Chapter 8 explores the role of community school partners through the lessons learned from Chicago Public Schools' Community School Initiative. Ray and Egner describe the way the district works with partners at the school site through a comprehensive quality improvement process.

We close the book in chapter 9 by examining the district's role in supporting work at the community school site. McArthur, Majors, and Noser outline Metropolitan Nashville Public School System's strategies to address the barriers to learning through the alignment of internal and external resources, and building district and school capacity.

Community schools are a collaborative education reform strategy that requires many hands working together toward a common vision. We hope that this book helps elucidate the uniqueness of each role and that you better understand the interconnectedness of each role to a successful community school. Ultimately, we hope that this book helps you discover your place in the growing community school movement.

REFERENCES

Coalition for Community Schools. (n.d.). Frequently asked questions about community schools. Retrieved December 8, 2009, from http://communityschools .org/index.php?option=content&task=view&id=6&Itemid=27.

Lubell, E., & Children's Aid Society. (2011). *Building community schools: A guide for action.* Children's Aid Society.

Maier, A., Daniel, J., Oakes, J., & Lam, L. (2017). *Community schools as an effective school improvement strategy: A review of the evidence.* Palo Alto, CA: Learning Policy Institute. Retrieved from https://learningpolicyinstitute.org/sites/default/files/product-files/Community_Schools_Effective_REPORT.pdf.

National Education Association. (2017). *The six pillars of community schools toolkit: NEA resource guide for educators, families, and communities.* Washington, D.C.

Chapter One

The Community Schools Movement

Emergence and Growth Trends

Reuben Jacobson

This book examines the many roles necessary for the effective implementation of a collaborative education reform strategy—the community school. As the founding director of the Coalition for Community Schools, Marty Blank, always said, community schools are a political enterprise—they are about relationships. They are about real people identifying real needs in a school and, working collaboratively in their roles, identifying assets, programs, and partners that meet those needs.

There is strength and power of relationships across roles. These relationships are built on trust that emerges from working together in a common cause. Those experiences, in turn, create the fertile ground of collaboration that enables the successful integration of educational, youth development, and community change opportunities.

The roles described throughout this book demonstrate how people build relationships through community schools in order to effect change. As more leaders from education, the community, families, faith-based institutions, higher education institutions, business, philanthropy, and nonprofits work together through the community school strategy, it's worth reflecting on where the community school movement came from, its current rise, what part leaders in different roles contributed, and what the future may hold.[1]

Individuals who have worked in high-poverty public schools have learned about the many other roles that impact a student's learning. Some of those roles, like teachers and principals, have a clear impact on students. However, there are also roles that are required to create real change, but are not sufficiently represented.

Schools need the leaders of community-based organizations, government agencies, faith-based institutions, and especially family and community members to partner with our schools and share ownership for what
types of opportunities our students receive. It's nearly impossible for any
one person to meet the needs of all children by themselves. As chapter
3 will demonstrate, every child should have an excellent teacher, but
sometimes that role alone is insufficient. Community schools unite these
individuals for student success.

The strength of the community school strategy is evidenced by the
growing body of research and years of effective practices. Community
schools are the types of schools that we need for the 21st century. They
are innovative while being rooted in a long history. They are the delivery
system for all that we ask schools to do, from mentoring to after-school to
family engagement and beyond, but resourced through partnerships to get
the job done. Rather than relying on unsustainable silver bullet programs
or solutions, community school leaders understand that schools alone
cannot address all the challenges our students face. We require a more
comprehensive whole school approach.

We turn now to a history of the community schools movement in order
to place this book and the roles described within it in a broader context
of leaders that have worked to bring schools and communities together.

A HISTORY OF COMMUNITY SCHOOLS
AND THE DIFFERENT ROLES OF
MOVEMENT LEADERS

Americans have always had a variety of ideas about what "schools"
should look like and what their purpose is. From our earliest days as
a country, however, our leaders believed in the need for and power of
schools to improve the lives of all citizens. Over time, schools have reflected the best and the worst of our society. For example, racist policies
demonstrated that schools could be used as a tool to segregate children
and reserve opportunities for advancement for a select group.

However, public schools that are available to all children have also
been at the core of our democracy. They have trained our leaders, scien-
tists, and innovators. They have helped millions of immigrants learn about

our country and receive academic training they may not have had the opportunity to receive in the countries of their birth.

Community schools are often thought of as schools that "do more" than the traditional school: more community involvement, more services for students and community members, and more democratic participation.[2] However, when you think about it, the school has always been a unique community institution that has served multiple purposes. From the very beginning of our formalized school system, Americans have taught their students more than just reading, writing, and arithmetic.

For example, in arguing for a system of public education for all children, Thomas Jefferson sought to develop citizens capable of taking leadership roles in a participatory democracy (Spring, 2001). While there may have initially been more emphasis on academic instruction, schools also taught morality, character development, health, and vocational training from their inception (Tyack, 1979).

The advent of the community school movement by Progressive Era leaders at the start of the 20th century took schools' multiple roles to a new level. According to John Rogers (1998), who developed one of the most nuanced analyses of the different waves of the community school movement over the last century, community schools have always served a number of purposes including providing health and other services, using the community as curriculum, and promoting democratic participation. Each successive generation of community schools has focused their specific purposes according to their social and historical context.

Rogers contends that community schools arise whenever social conditions call for school reform. He writes that there are three specific societal pressures that contribute to the rise of community schools in each time period: when the existing institutions can't meet the demands of society, when the community questions existing solutions and knowledge, and when the community sees a need to question the professionals charged with educating children. What follows is a summary describing the changes the community school movement has experienced over the past 100 years.

- **Progressive Era: Schools as Center and Expanding Services (1890–1920):** Progressive leaders established the foundational ideals upon which modern community schools stand. From Jane Addams and her settlement houses that provided myriad services to immigrants and the poor to John Dewey and his ideas about the power of schools to support communities, these leaders helped create the foundation for community schools. In addition to establishing the democratic features of the school as community center, reformers also used community schools to engage the needs of children as the economy and society rapidly developed.

- **The New Deal Era: Community-Based Curriculum for Community Problems (1930s):** Community schools rose again when society faced unprecedented problems such as poverty and unemployment during the Great Depression. Community schools moved from an emphasis on the center of the community to places where students and educators could solve pressing community problems. During this period, community school students and staff assessed the needs of the community, the resources available within the community, and then used the school to coordinate the delivery of services.
- **Quiet Development (World War II to the 1960s):** The time period between the Great Depression and the 1960s is characterized by the quiet development of community schools while the movement faced a number of threats including: the incorporation of support professionals into the educational bureaucracy, rather than coming from partner organizations; a focus on individual deficits, rather than systems approaches; and a focus on the growing suburbs, rather than urban and poor children (McMahon, Ward, Kline Pruett, Davidson, & Griffith, 2000).
- **The War on Poverty, Community Power, and Engagement (1960–1970):** The 1960s and early 1970s represented a renewed period of progressive reform in America. Rogers (1998) described two types of community schools that arose during the 1960s. The first were schools that focused on compensatory services as part of President Johnson's Great Society. Under this model, community schools had a functional approach: deliver services to improve the living conditions of this country's poor. In Rogers's second model, minorities in urban centers who were distrustful of the schools made arguments for greater community participation in decision making. Unlike the community school model of prior eras when professionals told the schools' "clients" what services and curriculum they needed, the community being served began

to have more power in the decisions being made about their services and education. This led to a direct conflict with the professionals who had been accustomed to making the decisions about how best to serve their clients since the Progressive Era (Rogers, 1998; Tyack, 1992).

• **The Contemporary Community Schools Movement (1994–Present):** While community schools have always included services, curricular connections to community, and community engagement, the contemporary community schools gained renewed prominence under the idea of integrating and providing services at the school site, what many refer to today as wraparound services or integrated student supports. Central to this rebirth was Joy Dryfoos's 1994 seminal book, *Full-Service Schools: A Revolution in Health and Social Services for Children, Youth, and Families*. With a variety of models similar to full-service schools around the country working to bring extra services into the schools along with community support, the time was ripe for a new community school movement. Dryfoos and leaders from the Children's Aid Society (now called Children's Aid), a New York City settlement house, and the University of Pennsylvania's Center for Community Partnerships decided that they needed to jump-start a community school movement, a "comprehensive vision to unite its [community schools'] various models and a vehicle to advance its message" (Blank, 2005, p. 246). After a small convening, a working group decided to create a coalition of national, state, and local organizations that ascribed to community school ideals. The Institute for Educational Leadership (IEL) offered to staff the effort. The strength of the Emerging Coalition for Community Schools (as it was called) would be that a network of partners would have ownership of the movement. This theory of action has proven to be very effective as described in other sections that characterize the growing activity of Coalition for Community Schools ("the Coalition") partners. Together with practitioners, capacity builders, and other leaders across the country, the Coalition has helped grow the community schools movement over the past 20 years.

Building on a rich history, leaders have continued to grow the community school movement, as described in the following section.

CURRENT GROWTH OF THE
COMMUNITY SCHOOL MOVEMENT

The community schools movement has grown in important ways over the past 20 years. The exact number of community schools is difficult to measure since community schools look different in each state, city, district, and school site. Overall, community school leaders have estimated that there are over 5,000 community schools in the United States (Blank & Villarreal, 2015).

Growth of community schools happened during a period where accountability was the dominant education reform strategy. The federal No Child Left Behind law was created in 2001 and had an emphasis on high-stakes accountability that would identify "failing" schools and require a narrow set of "turnaround" strategies that districts would be required to implement. These "top-down" strategies are in stark contrast to the community schools that developed during that time, mostly from the ground-up as community-driven solutions to school reform. That is not to say that community schools didn't focus on academic outcomes, they certainly did. However, they also developed shared accountability with partners through locally driven solutions.

There are a variety of explanations for why city, county, school district, state, and community leaders have been growing community schools over the last 20 years. Increases in poverty rates, the need for new approaches to education reform, local demand from communities, new approaches to including partners inside the school, better examples of success that others can learn from, new leaders and policies, better research, and political support are all possible contributing factors. It is likely that each of these reasons contributed to the growth in community schools and we turn to a more thorough consideration of each next.

Growing Needs

Shifting demographics and greater demands in public schools are likely reasons for the increased interest in community schools as a strategy to support students and families in need, similar to earlier eras. The Southern Education Foundation found that in 2013, over half of the students in public schools were identified as low-income (Southern Education Foundation, 2015). Poverty brings a host of related challenges such as poor health, hunger, homelessness, and safety that all impact student learning (Basch, 2011; Rothstein, 2004).

Schools have limited capacity to address these issues on their own. Resources in the community, the social safety net, are limited as well. Poverty, of course, isn't restricted to urban centers. One report describes child poverty in rural areas as an "emergency," noting that nearly 25 percent of rural children are poor (Save the Children, 2018). Suburban poverty has grown as well (Kneebone, 2017). This leaves all types of school districts confronting new challenges and looking for new solutions. Community schools have risen as a response to the challenges of poverty.

Local Leaders Promoting Community Schools as a Cross-Sector Approach

Community schools may be started by a variety of institutions including nonprofits, foundations, United Ways, and universities. In fact, these organizations "outside" of the school system are primarily responsible for the resurgence of community schools in the 1990s and early 2000s. However, over the past 10 years, school district superintendents and mayors who have greater responsibility and authority for schools have leveraged their leadership positions and have made a highly visible impact on the growth of community schools. These local leaders decided to use the community school strategy to address the growing needs in schools combined with their limited resources. District and city leaders have given greater visibility to the community school strategy.

School district leaders increasingly see the value in community schools and have made them a part of their district's strategic plans. One of the first was Chicago Public Schools' chief executive officer Arne Duncan (who later became President Obama's secretary of education) who took a community school pilot initiative by the Polk Bros. Foundation and set a goal of launching 100 community schools within five years. More than 15 years later, that community school initiative is still operating in Chicago, as described in chapter 8.

A milestone was the transformation of Oakland Unified School District into a "community school district." In 2010 Superintendent Tony Smith, who is currently the Illinois State Superintendent of Education, worked with his staff and the community to create a scaled up community school strategy to address the inequities in the school system, confront issues of poverty that impacted student success, and create better learning opportunities for all students.

Through a comprehensive engagement process, Smith and other Oakland leaders created a robust district-wide community schools initiative that is supported by a school board policy. The district has even changed its tagline to "Oakland Unified School District—Community Schools, Thriving Students." Kendra Fehrer and Aurora Lopez describe the Oakland story in greater detail in chapter 7.

Mayors have also begun to make significant investments in community schools. In New York City, current mayor Bill de Blasio has helped grow community schools significantly. In 2013 the New York City teachers' union, the United Federation of Teachers, took all the mayoral candidates to Cincinnati, Ohio, to visit an exemplar community school site and initiative. After visiting Oyler Community Learning Center (the name Cincinnati gives to its community schools), candidate de Blasio told the *New York Times* that he saw "endless potential" in the approach and according to the newspaper, he and other candidates made community schools "a centerpiece of their campaigns" (Hernández, 2013).

At the same time, local organizers like the Coalition for Educational Justice were building ground-level support for community schools. In June 2014, just five months after Mayor de Blasio took office, he repurposed $52 million to create 40 community schools. He also created an Office of Community Schools. During the 2018–2019 school year, the mayor's initiative supported 227 community schools that partner with 62 lead nonprofit community organizations with a total budget of $195 million per year.

The community school strategy is not limited to our nation's largest school districts. Superintendents and elected officials in places as diverse as Vancouver, Washington; Newark, New Jersey; Cincinnati, Ohio; Grand Rapids, Michigan; Evansville, Indiana; Portland, Oregon; Las Vegas, Nevada; Hayward, California; Philadelphia, Pennsylvania; Nashville, Tennessee; and Milwaukee, Wisconsin; have all helped create community schools in their cities.

Growth of More Comprehensive and Collaborative Approaches to Education Reform

Another explanation for the growth of community schools is frustration with narrow approaches to education reform and the accountability movement more generally. Entire books have been written about failed efforts to improve outcomes for schools through various school reforms that capture a lot of attention and resources and focus on narrow approaches—and then fail (Noddings, 2007; Payne, 2008; Ravitch, 2001).

As Linda Darling-Hammond and Chris Edly write, "waves of 'reforms' . . . have failed to fill the deep fractures in quality of life and access to opportunity that run along racial, economic, and geographic lines." In contrast, they go on to write that

> many community schools, including both district-run schools and some public charter schools, show promise as vehicles for using these strategies to improve student opportunities and outcomes and help counteract the impact of multigenerational disinvestment in low-income communities and communities of color (Edley, Jr. & Darling-Hammond, 2018).

More comprehensive, whole child, and place-based approaches have emerged over the past 10 years. Leaders in local communities have been working on comprehensive strategies such as the neighborhood-based Harlem Children's Zone, collective impact approaches, and community schools. Sometimes described as "place-based initiatives," these types of strategies attended to the numerous factors impacting student success and organized resources to support students and families.

The Obama administration helped accelerate the development of these approaches by supporting "place-based" efforts through funding and greater visibility. Using the Harlem Children's Zone as a model, the administration created the Promise Neighborhoods Initiative at the U.S. Department of Education. As of 2018, the department has awarded 71 grants that help communities create supportive services from early childhood education to after-school activities to job training programs.

Outside government, cross-sector approaches (sometimes referred to as "collective impact") have also grown as a way to unite systems in a comprehensive and collaborative way to address educational inequities (Henig, Riehl, Houston, Rebell, & Wolff, 2016). Examples such as

StriveTogether, Communities in Schools, the Coalition for Community Schools, Promise Neighborhoods, and Say Yes to Education have all helped change the conversation in education reform.

Unions, Organizers, and Families Have Helped Build Demand

While community schools have benefited from support by elected officials, they have also benefited from demand by unions, community organizers, and families. In fact, it's likely that elected officials took action as a result of organizers mobilizing communities to call for community schools. A few examples illustrate their role.

An early member of the Coalition for Community Schools, the American Federation of Teachers dramatically increased its role in the community schools movement in 2008, when newly elected American Federation of Teachers (AFT) president, Randi Weingarten, called for the rapid growth of community schools in her inaugural address. Weingarten asked, "Can you imagine a federal law that promoted *community schools*—schools that serve the neediest children by bringing together under one roof all the services and activities they and their families need?" ("Randi Weingarten AFT Convention Speech," 2008). Since 2008, the AFT has dedicated staff, resources, and communications to promote the community school strategy including through magazines for their 1.1 million members on the approach and innovation grants.

The National Education Association (NEA), which represents three million members, has also become an increasingly vocal supporter of community schools. Their president, Lily Eskelsen García, has written and spoken about advancing community schools. In an interview with a local newspaper in New Mexico, Eskelsen García says, "Community schools are generally interested in beefing up the academic programs, but also offering more electives—music, sports, clubs and field trips. The kinds of things that make school really interesting come back, because everything is planned by the school community" (Willis, 2007).

The NEA has a dedicated website and staff working on community schools, and has held institutes for their local unions to learn more about the strategy and to advance policies in their communities. Significantly, the NEA's 2018 Representative Assembly passed a policy statement in support of community schools, only the eighth policy statement in the organization's 160-year history.

Community organizers across the country have also made the demand for community schools central to their education reform platforms, sometimes as a response to the growth of charters. The Journey for Justice Alliance (JFJ) is an alliance of community-based organizations in 24 cities and is led by Jitu Brown, a former community school coordinator in Chicago's Kenwood Oakland neighborhood. Together with other local organizing groups, JFJ, the unions, and others created the Alliance to Reclaim our Schools (AROS), whose platform calls for 10,000 sustainable community schools.

Whereas in previous eras the community was often left out of the development and implementation of community schools, today's era is characterized by notable expansion of the role organizers, unions, and families play in the community school movement at multiple levels. Hester and Capers write more about the role of family and community organizing in chapter 6.

Advocates Have Developed Supportive Policies at Multiple Levels

Advocates for community schools have promoted supportive policy at the federal, state, and local levels that have helped the community school movement grow and gain greater recognition as a school reform strategy. In 2018, the Partnership for the Future of Learning compiled featured examples of community schools policies to create the "Community Schools Playbook," so that advocates can continue to advance supportive policies (Partnership for the Future of Learning, 2018).

Federal Policy

Representative Steny Hoyer of the State of Maryland introduced the first federal Full-Service Community Schools Act in Congress in 2004 and reintroduced it multiple times before it was finally approved in 2009. The bill created a new Full-Service Community Schools program in the U.S. Department of Education that would award competitive grants to communities. According to the U.S. Department of Education, since 2009, the program has been appropriated $55,000,000 and awarded 32 grants in competitions in 2010, 2014, and 2015. Most recently, in yet another sign of the growth of the movement, Congress appropriated $17.5 million for fiscal year 2018 to support the grant program, an increase of $7.5 million.

In addition to the grant program, Congress included Full-Service Community Schools in the Every Student Succeeds Act (ESSA), a reauthorization of the Elementary and Secondary Education Act. The Full-Service Community Schools program became authorized under a subpart labeled "Community Support for Student Success," making it a part of the federal education law, and not another program that would have to get introduced in future Congresses. This language has codified community schools in federal law.

While not the only federal source for community schools (e.g., 21st Century Community Learning Centers have always represented a significant funding stream for community schools), these important markers represent greater recognition of the community school approach.

ESSA has also been a signal to the education community that there should be greater focus on local approaches that engage a variety of stakeholders in making decisions about how schools should operate and what they would be accountable for. Each state is required to create state plans as part of ESSA that engage local stakeholders. State officials have solicited input by holding meetings in communities across their state as well as collecting input online. This approach to engaging the community is consistent with the community school strategy. Various states have referred to efforts similar to community schools in their plans and some, such as Pennsylvania, specifically promote the strategy.

State Policy

While ESSA codified community schools at the federal level, a number of state policies crafted before and after ESSA passage have helped grow community schools as well. Approximately 16 states have either introduced or passed community school policies since 2016.

Local Policy

A number of local cities, counties, and school districts have introduced policies to support community schools. Community members, families, organizers, and unions have advocated for these policies. The specific policies represent a wide variety of approaches, from calling for district-wide adoption of the community school strategy to supporting the creation of a handful of community schools. These policies have helped solidify and sustain community schools, enabling them to grow with the official support of local governing bodies such as school boards.[3]

Growing Body of Research Provides Credibility

Community schools are intentionally designed to be a results-based strategy that changes outcomes for students and families. While community schools, like other complex and comprehensive approaches, are difficult to evaluate because of their many moving parts and variety of programs, new research is making the case that they are effective and achieving improved outcomes.

Perhaps the most significant analysis of the community schools research is a 2017 report from the Learning Policy Institute and the National Education Policy Center, titled *Community Schools as an Effective School Improvement Strategy: A Review of the Evidence* (Maier, Daniel, Oakes, & Lam, 2017). Looking at over 150 studies, the researchers conclude that community schools are an evidence-based practice by the standards for evidence set out in the federal Every Student Succeeds Act and that the research points toward positive outcomes.

More local initiatives are also teaming up with researchers to ensure they are using data for continuous improvement and evaluation. Think tanks such as the Center for American Progress, the Brookings Institution, and the Learning Policy Institute have also written about community schools, raising their visibility among researchers and policy makers. In addition, the Coalition for Community Schools convenes a group of researchers interested in the community school strategy from universities, think tanks, and evaluation companies. There are still many research questions about this complex strategy and a need to identify impact over time. Researchers, perhaps yet another role in the community school movement, are organized to develop and implement a research agenda to answer these questions.

A Sustainable Education Reform Strategy

Finally, communities are mobilizing to solve local problems with locally developed solutions. Knowing that a narrow approach dictated by policy makers from outside the community is insufficient, these local leaders are working collaboratively to create sustainable "home grown" strategies like community schools. Community schools also benefit from diversified and collaborative leadership that help sustain the approach. Initiatives with diversified leadership build a broader base of support that can sustain the initiative when leadership changes.

As we argue in this book, a variety of practitioners must become leaders and work together to create a transformational community school. If schools are to return to their role as democratic centers of our community through the community school strategy (Dionne, Jr., Ornstein, & Mann, 2017), then we need more people representing a diverse group of stakeholders interested in our schools to be a part of education reform moving forward. The community school strategy works because everyone shares in collaborative leadership and responsibility for what happens at the school site and systems levels.

CHALLENGES

Community schools have grown over the past 20 years and are becoming more broadly accepted as a mainstream and evidence-based educational reform strategy, however, challenges remain at multiple levels. As this chapter demonstrates, interest in community schools, like other education reform strategies, waxes and wanes over time. Community schools need to maintain their relevance and establish themselves as a mainstream education and community change approach in order to break that cycle and keep their momentum.

In order to do that, community schools must continue to demonstrate their impact. Policy makers, funders, and school leaders at all levels require that investments in education produce results for students. Simply put, community schools must show impact on student learning in order for a principal to buy in to the strategy. Relatedly, community schools require data from multiple sectors and data sharing presents a host of technical and political challenges. Community school practitioners are working together with related collaborative educational approaches to address obstacles to data sharing.

Funding of community schools is a constant challenge. Currently, community schools are funded by a variety of sources, oftentimes from competitive grants or philanthropy. Those sources often change whom they are giving their resources to and the types of strategies they support change frequently as well. Federal dollars for community schools provide a limited set of resources only to a very few grantees. Community schools will likely always use a portfolio approach of pulling together a variety of resources. However, identifying consistent and sustainable funding to support the core roles and structures of the community school, such as the community school coordinator, is incumbent upon movement leaders.

Sustainability isn't only a funding issue. Leaders from multiple levels, including principals, mayors, and superintendents, have demonstrated their support for community schools. However, people in leadership roles change frequently and the priorities of future leaders may not match up.

Developing a diverse set of leaders who can maintain the strategy when one leader departs, or when priorities change, is a challenge for the field. Similarly, community schools operate in a congested educational reform space. Many different approaches, some closely related to community schools, others using some of the programmatic elements, are competing for limited attention and resources. Identifying ways to work together with these other approaches while maintaining required features is a challenge for community schools.

Developing community ownership is another challenge. Schools that simply integrate services are important and provide needed supports for students and their families. Those schools, however, are different than the more developed full-service community schools that the current community schools movement seeks (Valli, Stefanski, & Jacobson, 2014). Today's community schools require family and community ownership as key elements of the strategy. However, caregivers are busy, not every community has organizers working to support the approach, and sometimes the school and service professionals continue to assume they know what's best, as we saw in earlier eras. Family and community engagement is challenging, but it helps sustain the community school and is a critical implementation element of every community school.

FINAL THOUGHTS

Community schools have a long history, have gone through multiple iterations, and have grown over the past 20 years. It's useful to think about what's next for the community schools field as we begin to explore the various roles that are described in the following chapters.

We are beginning to reach a tipping point where community schools are becoming more mainstream—a permanent part of the education and community landscape. Now that the education field is looking more broadly at the needs of the whole child, from trauma-informed care and mental health services, to youth development and connections to work, policy makers, researchers, and the media are more often discussing community schools as a recognized education reform strategy. With greater recognition and acceptance, more schools and school districts are likely to create community school initiatives, further solidifying their role as a mainstream educational reform strategy.

We are going to see more local community school initiatives launch at the district level. District and community leaders are searching for new approaches and recognize they need results-focused and aligned partners to support a robust education system. A new generation of district leaders is likely to look to the community school strategy as the new normal about the way schools should operate.

Over the past five years, a number of state-level coalitions supporting community schools have developed. Guided by the Coalition for Community Schools, state coalitions from Wisconsin to California to Texas have worked to improve implementation of community schools, build a strong message about their value, and advocated for and advanced community school policies. More states will create these coalitions that will in turn lead to more community schools and the need for more state-level roles to support the approach.

"Quality" has become increasingly important to the future growth of community schools. As a field, we knew that a quality community school has a strong coordinator, a supportive principal, and strong stakeholder engagement—especially from parents. Over the past few years, the Coalition for Community Schools worked with partners to develop "community school standards" that are based on the experiences of practitioners across the country. That effort has helped inform what a quality community school should look like and has implications for each of the roles described in the chapters that follow. Attention to quality community schools will continue to grow.

As the community schools approach receives greater recognition, and greater scrutiny, it is incumbent upon the field to pay attention to high-quality implementation of community schools in order to secure results (Maier et al., 2017). Part of that quality agenda requires even better research on the implementation and outcomes of community schools.

Community schools are an education reform strategy on the rise. The field continues to grow champions at every level. Funders are increasingly looking at strategies that are more inclusive of partnerships and engagement. Most important, local communities are claiming greater responsibility and ownership for educational approaches that maximize local assets and are responsive to the needs of families and youth living in complex environments. This chapter has demonstrated that the community school field is thriving. Its continued success relies in no small measure on the significant roles described next.

REFERENCES

Maier, A., Daniel, J., Oakes, J., & Lam, L. (2017). *Community schools as an effective school improvement strategy: A review of the evidence.* Palo Alto, CA: Learning Policy Institute. Retrieved from https://learningpolicyinstitute.org/sites/default/files/product-files/Community_Schools_Effective_REPORT.pdf.

Basch, C. E. (2011). Healthier students are better learners: High-Quality, strategically planned, and effectively coordinated school health programs must be a fundamental mission of schools to help close the achievement gap. *Journal of School Health, 81*(10), 650–662. https://doi.org/10.1111/j.1746-1561.2011.00640.x.

Blank, M. J. (2005). Reaching out to create a movement. In J. G. Dryfoos, J. Quinn, & C. Barkin (Eds.), *Community schools in action: Lessons from a decade of practice* (pp. 243–258). New York: Oxford University Press.

Blank, M. J., & Villarreal, L. (2015). Where it all comes together: How partnerships connect communities and schools. *American Educator, 39*(3), 4.

Dionne, Jr., E. J., Ornstein, N. J., & Mann, T. E. (2017). *One nation after Trump: A guide for the perplexed, the disillusioned, the desperate, and the not-yet deported.* New York: St. Martin's Press.

Edley, Jr., C., & Darling-Hammond, L. (2018, August 16). Community schools: A powerful strategy to disrupt inequitable systems. Retrieved September 5, 2018, from https://learningpolicyinstitute.org/blog/community-schools-powerful-strategy-disrupt-inequitable-systems.

Hernández, J. C. (2013, August 11). Mayoral candidates see Cincinnati as a model for New York schools. *The New York Times.* Retrieved from https://

www.nytimes.com/2013/08/12/nyregion/candidates-see-cincinnati-as-model
-for-new-york-schools.html.

Henig, J. R., Riehl, C. J., Houston, D. M., Rebell, M. A., & Wolff, J. R. (2016). *Collective impact and the new generation of cross-sector collaborations for education: A nationwide scan.* New York: Teachers College, Columbia University. Retrieved from http://www.tc.columbia.edu/education-policy-and -social-analysis/.

Kneebone, E. (2017). The changing geography of U.S. poverty, § House Ways and Means Committee, Subcommittee on Human Resources. Washington, D.C.: The Brookings Institution. Retrieved from https://www.brookings.edu /testimonies/the-changing-geography-of-us-poverty/.

McMahon, T. J., Ward, N. L., Kline Pruett, M., Davidson, L., & Griffith, E. E. H. (2000). Building full-service schools: Lessons learned in the development of interagency collaboratives. *Journal of Educational & Psychological Consulta- tion, 11*(1), 65–92.

Noddings, N. (2007). *When school reform goes wrong.* New York: Teachers College Press.

Partnership for the Future of Learning. (2018). *Community schools playbook.* Retrieved from http://communityschools.futureforlearning.org/.

Payne, C. M. (2008). *So much reform, so little change: The persistence of failure in urban schools.* Cambridge, MA: Harvard Education Press.

Ravitch, D. (2001). *Left back: A century of battles over school reform.* New York: Simon & Schuster.

Rogers, J. S. (1998). *Community schools: Lessons for the past and present.* Flint, MI: Charles S. Mott Foundation.

Rothstein, R. (2004). *Class and schools: Using social, economic, and educa- tional reform to close the black-white achievement gap.* New York: Teachers College, Columbia University; Economic Policy Institute.

Save the Children. (2018). *Growing up rural in America.* Fairfield, CT: Save the Children. Retrieved from https://www.savethechildren.org/content/dam /global/reports/2018-end-of-childhood-report-us.pdf.

Southern Education Foundation. (2015). *Research bulletin: A new majority low income students now a majority in the nation's public schools.* Atlanta, GA. Retrieved from http://www.southerneducation.org/getattachment/4ac62e27 -5260-47a5-9d02-14896ec3a531/A-New-Majority-2015-Update-Low-Income -Students-Now.aspx.

Spring, J. H. (2001). *The American school, 1642–2000.* Boston: McGraw-Hill.

Tyack, D. (1979). The high school as a social service agency: Historical perspec- tives on current policy issues. *Educational Evaluation and Policy Analysis, 1*(5), 45–57.

Tyack, D. (1992). Health and social services in public schools: Historical Perspectives. *The future of children: School-Linked services, 2*(1), 19–31.

Valli, L., Stefanski, A., & Jacobson, R. (2014). Typologizing school–community partnerships: A framework for analysis and action. *Urban Education,* 0042085914549366. https://doi.org/10.1177/0042085914549366.

Weingarten, R. AFT convention speech. (2008, July 14). Retrieved from http://www.aft.org/convention/releases/weingarten071408.pdf.

Willis, D. (2007, January 19). Q&A: NEA President Lily Eskelsen Garcia. *Las Cruces Sun-News.* Retrieved from https://www.lcsun-news.com/story/news/education/lcps/2017/01/19/q-nea-president-lily-eskelsen-garcia/96814690.

Chapter Two

The Imagineers[1] of Community School Leadership

Lynda Tredway and Matthew Militello

Community schools have dramatically changed the way "we do school." Now recognized as a vital national reform effort, community schools re-imagine what schools require to ensure student attainment by focusing on a balanced set of school goals that include academic success, physical and emotional health, and civic and community readiness.[2] An important adjunct to what community schools urge us to do is the Community Learning Exchange (CLE) reform effort, which offers a robust set of processes to address the elusive *how*—how to enact community schools in ways that fully involve the students and families who are most affected by the projected outcomes.

Community Learning Exchanges (CLEs) view school change as an emulsion process in which we work slowly and steadily with contextual ingredients—people, place, time, and interactions—toward deep and lasting reform: the slow drip of building relational trust to engage together in designing and implementing the kinds of schools that involve the entire community as learners and leaders.

CLEs share with community schools a sustained confidence in Dewey's criteria of experience, viewing the importance of an experiential continuum and focused interactions as a foundation for organizational change and improvement. As Dewey (1938) asks of us: "Does this form of growth create conditions for further growth?" (p. 36).

We subscribe to this CLE premise: trust the generative themes that emerge from each unique context (Freire, 1970) to advance the school in each community as a center of building academic, social-emotional, and civic outcomes for students. As the generative themes for the community's direction become apparent from participant dialogue in circles, learning walks, and storytelling, CLE facilitators use the emergent themes for encouraging and sustaining all-important relational trust, a prerequisite building block of durable school reform efforts.

Exchange is the operative word; by selecting processes that foster continuous dialogue, the goal of full reciprocity between and among all constituents (parents, students, teachers, and administrators) in school and district reform efforts is tangible and observable. As one CLE participant said in a closing circle:[3] "I had no idea we could get this deep this fast and tell stories that help us move our school forward." Thus, the CLE theory of action offers a critical frame for rethinking the *power of place* and the *wisdom of people* as key foci for any plan of action in a school, district, or organization (Guajardo, Guajardo, Janson, & Militello, 2016).

In this chapter, authors see how school leadership is a critical linchpin of community school implementation and how two leaders practice the key tenets of community schools and Community Learning Exchanges. The leadership stories told in this chapter bring to life the ways the complementary frameworks of community schools and Community Learning Exchange support equitable, community-based school reform.

The criteria for successful community schools comport with the Community Learning Exchange axioms or propositions (see table 2.1). The complementary reform efforts have taken root precisely because they offer theories of action, strategies, and pedagogies that make sense to people in local contexts and mirror the ways we want all school constituents to take charge of their local contexts for building and sustaining reform. The authors of this chapter are active in both networks: community schools and Community Learning Exchanges. Both these efforts require determined and shared leadership (Spillane, 2006; Spillane & Coldren, 2011).

We share stories of two community school principals whose visionary leadership is driven by their commitment to equitable school outcomes. They are linchpins in their school reform efforts, and their courage inspires others to co-imagine a different path forward. What comes to mind in their stories is Walt Disney's Imagineers—groups of people who innovate by paying attention to the interplay of intuition, experience, knowledge, and skill. As creative leaders, they catalyze the collective spirit of others to re-imagine schools and communities as places of hope and possibility (Nachmanovitch, 1993).

To some degree, however, this chapter is also a cautionary tale about what it takes to systematically think about and do in order to design, implement, monitor, and celebrate community schools. The experiences and decisions of the principals we feature are not formulas to be scaled; rather, they offer ideas about community school leadership that stimulate and inform possibilities for you and your school. The tale starts with taking a look at the crosswalk between the criteria for successful community schools, the Community Learning Exchange axioms, and practices of community schools and Community Learning Exchanges (see table 2.1) that exemplify these frameworks.

As we proceed to the principals' stories in their community schools, we invite you to visualize how the criteria and axioms resonate with you and offer a way forward for your school, district, and community.

Community schools continue to fight against inequities and foster principles and services that support schools, school districts, and the adults and children who are in them (Dryfoos & Maguire, 2002; Dryfoos, Quinn, & Barkin, 2005; Henderson, Mapp, Johnson & Davies, 2007; Epstein, Sanders, & Simon, 2008). The necessary services include: extending the school day; addressing health and wellness at school sites; fully involving parents as partners in decisions and actions; being fully knowledgeable about the home lives of their students; and working with other community organizations and constituents to enrich and support teaching and learning. The key component of all that action is *how the adults organize themselves to ensure equity, reciprocity, and purpose.*

Community Learning Exchanges—national, regional, and local one to four day "events" in which intergenerational teams (teachers, school leaders, parents, youth, elders and community organizers, and service providers)—develop collective capacity to engage in community-informed reform such as community schools. Community Learning Exchange axioms build on the belief that reform happens from the inside-out and that, given the autonomy and resources to do so, local constituents can and do make good decisions for their school communities (Guajardo et al., 2016; Grubb & Tredway, 2010). Moreover, Community Learning Exchanges provide practical strategies to bring the criteria of successful community schools and the CLE axioms to life.[4]

Table 2.1. Crosswalk: Community Schools Criteria and Community Learning Exchange Axioms

Community Schools Criteria	Community Learning Exchange Axioms	How the criteria and axioms are often manifested in *Community Schools*[1]
Engaging Students and Adults in their Learning Emphasizing High-Quality Teaching, not High-Stakes Testing	Learning and leadership are a dynamic social process	• Emphasis on high-quality teaching, not on high-stakes testing • Engaging, culturally relevant, and challenging curricula • Positive disciplinary practices, i.e., restorative justice, focus on self-regulation and cultivating respectful discipline systems, collective responsibility for healthy climate and culture • Supporting practices to reduce suspensions and address chronic absenteeism and eliminating harsh punishment, including data systems that track progress
Using Culturally Responsive Curricula, Discipline Practices, Pedagogy and Processes	Conversations are critical and central curricular and pedagogical processes	• Community/family meetings reflect the cultural practices of the community • Student voice in decision making • Parent/family learning opportunities that respond to parent/family decisions about what they need to know or do • Inclusion of parents and community members in teaching and learning practices in the classroom setting • Social Emotional Learning (SEL) curricula is instituted and effectiveness evidence is one criterion of school success

Implementing Wraparound Supports and Opportunities for Students and Adults	The people closest to the issues are best situated to discover answers to local concerns	• Processes and practices that ensure the voices and ideas of parents and community members become infused in the design and work of the school • Asset and equity-based inventories • Wraparound supports and opportunities that are co-designed and co-decided and managed with input from constituents • Community School Coordinator who has trusting relationships with students, parents, and community • Linked Day: Overlap and communication between school day teachers and after-school staff • Developing teacher and counselor pipelines for adults who work in aftercare program
Ensuring Shared and Inclusive Leadership	Crossing boundaries enriches development and the educational process	• Inclusive school leadership, including a community school coordinator • Authentic parent and community engagement • Cross walk between day school and after-school • Purposefully fostering community-based leadership • Intentional intergenerational leadership by honoring the often marginalized of youth and elders
Using the Wisdom of People and Power of Place as Guideposts for Change	Hopes and change are built on assets and dreams of locals and their communities	• Dynamic and equitable partnerships with organizations, students, parents, families, and caregivers in which all voices are honored • Collaborating with community members to learn the context and history of place; through community, historical and cultural mapping, fully engaging with community assets and community griots (those who carry the history and knowledge)

1. http://www.southerneducation.org/Publications/Community-Schools-Layout_021116.aspx

THE TALES OF TWO IMAGINEER
SCHOOL PRINCIPALS

*What the best and wisest parent wants for his child, that must we want
for all the children of the community. Anything less is unlovely, and left
unchecked, destroys our democracy.*

—John Dewey in *School and Society*, 1902

John Dewey's quote informs the vision, messaging, and practice of community school's principal leaders. Achieving the elusive "all" is complex
when some schools and students in those schools require more resources
to even approach parity. Parents, staff, and children may commit to "all,"
and that may be touted as a school or district goal. However, achieving
the goal is more complicated in actual practice, particularly in schools in
which students and families experience deep economic disparities.

The two schools described, and their dynamic leaders, have been at this
work of school reform and community school leadership for many years.
They recognize that change takes time and that sustaining relational trust,
dialogue, and authentic reciprocity are indispensable prerequisites for changing school culture and climate. They have systematically activated teams
of adults and youth to achieve durable outcomes in academics, citizenship,
and social-emotional learning. They know how to partner in strategic ways
with community school coordinators to build and ensure coherence and they
value the coordinator's essential role in the daily operations of the school.

Both principals are graduates of the preparation program for school
leaders at the University of California at Berkeley, which stresses equity
as an overarching goal of all leader actions and includes attention to
community schools and community mapping projects as a centerpiece
of its curriculum.

As veteran administrators in urban districts, the principals advocate
for and engage the community of teachers, support staff, children, youth,
and families. The principals' stories offer a window into how community
school leaders ensure the elusive "all." School One is a redesigned K–8
school, and the principal is an experienced teacher and school leader.
In School Two, the principal is committed to a tenure of 10 years at the
school, and he won the Coalition for Community Schools' Educator of the
Year award in 2018.

While these leaders cite the importance of collaborative and inclusive leadership in their schools, their work supports what research and practice has been clear about: *the school principal and other key leaders are critical to the success of a community school* (Jacobson, Hodges, & Blank, 2011).

School One and Principal Agustín

As Mr. Agustín walks through the neighborhood to get tea, we have an informal chat about how he is—which can only be termed exuberant. He talks about building on his prior experience in a K–5 community school to re-imagine how the merged K–8 school can be a full-service community school. The principal cut his teeth in school leadership and collaboration through multiple roles at an elementary school: instructional coach, assistant principal, and then principal. That school, designated as a community school when the district's strategic plan supported community schools, won the 2012 award as an exemplary community school from the Coalition of Community Schools.[5]

By the second year at the K–8, he pushed for a wall-to-wall community school. He is clear about the "why" of a community school: "When a parent drops a kid off, they need to know we have a common set of expectations and there needs to be alignment between the day program and the afterschool."

Principal Agustín views particular resources as foundational to academic progress. About his former school, he said, "Once we were calm [through using Caring School Community as curriculum for social-emotional learning], then we could move onto rigorous literacy—reading and writing workshop approach (using Lucy Calkins's approach)."[6] Concurrent with focusing on culture and climate was building a stronger relationship between the after-school program and the day program. He stated, "I saw a line worker in the after-school program as especially successful with kids and hired him as After-school Coordinator. Together we worked to link the after-school to the day school so that it was seamless."

Changing the after-school staff's workday so that it overlapped with day school, the after-school instructors interacted with teachers and could offer a program that continued the day school program. By merging day school with after-school into one seamless community school, he was able to create a pipeline for new teachers from after-school workers and leveraged opportunities related to internal district and external support. As a result, the K–5 school was a nationally award-winning school.

By transferring what he did at the previous school to the K–8 setting and instituting what he calls a linked-day program, the school is open from 7:30 a.m. to 6:00 p.m. Three leadership actions are key to his success and vision:

1. Developing abstract resources by deepening staff relationships and changing the use of time so teachers had more collaboration opportunities (Grubb, 2009);[7]
2. Choosing strong partners for after-school and social-emotional learning; and
3. Changing the leadership team structures, including making certain that the after-school coordinator is on the school leadership team.

First, he had to expand adult capacity—after-school, day school, support staff, and families—to be in regular communication and deepen their trust with each other. Abstract resources—people and their relationships and the ways they use their time—are cocreated and undergird a rigorous academic program.

Through his efforts, a grant helps the school re-imagine time and space and increase cultural competence and multilingual access: three-hour block periods for each grade level (K–5) to maximize teachers' time for "reflective practice and collaboration"; stronger student enrichment experience in art and health and wellness; linked-day staff from the community-based organization partnership to address youth development; and academic and social-emotional development support for long-term and newcomer English learners.

The second important factor is the choice of after-school partners. In his role at the elementary school, through strategic conversations, he worked to change the ways the after-school and day school staff communicated by changing the workday of the after-school staff. By writing grants and using the Caring School Communities curriculum,[8] the school created the all-important culture and climate that were needed to be present before fully addressing the academic program.

In a "listening tour" at his new school, Principal Agustín talked with teachers, current service providers, families, and youth (Safir, 2017). Then he planned a set of strategic actions: hiring a social worker (the after-school coordinator at his previous school who had completed an MSW program); changing the after-school provider by using the district guideline; inviting the district's after-school director to talk to staff and parents; and arranging for providers to present at all parent meetings. The result: a community-based organization that holds the same values and supports the work and the seamless connection between day and after-school.

Finally, recognizing that leadership is a function, not only a person, he consistently builds structures for shared leadership and responsibility. He expanded the bimonthly lead team meetings to include teachers and, on alternating weeks, a community school team meets to support culture and climate and links to after-school program and parent partnerships. That team analyzes the youth development framework that asks this fundamental question: *What is appropriate autonomy and accountability for youth in middle school?* Relying on that framework has provided another leverage point for his actions and choices, including his next action: choosing a stronger social-emotional learning curriculum called Second Step.

The linked day provides an additional benefit by serving as a pipeline for potential teachers, a chronic need in the district. By the time Principal Agustín left the first elementary school, the linked day program became integral to how the school functioned; at budget meetings each spring with the School Site Council, the money for this approach was never on the chopping block.

In the K–8 school, the CEO of a local company has offered middle schools increasingly larger grants for improving their capacity and outcomes. The school applied for and received that grant, and Principal Agustín's entrepreneurial ability lends cache and credibility to his leadership actions.[9] There is more to come at this school, but the groundwork he laid provides the structure, improved culture and climate, and secured funding for moving ahead to ensure solid academic, social-emotional, and civic outcomes for students.

School Two and Principal Hong

Principal Hong greets visitors at Roosevelt Middle School with a big smile and tells a story about what is wonderful today at the school. On his office bulletin board hangs his personal standard: *Would I want Yuji or Tomu (his sons) to attend Roosevelt today?* He is a recognized leader in this district.[10] He jump-starts the conversation by detailing two frames that guide his decisions: technical and moral/ethical. As the conversation unfolds, he has command of mantras that guide him, and the first one is a truism: *What you measure is what gets done.* Thus, he even revises the typical technical frame by using metrics that buttress his values and measure the right evidence at the right time in the reform trajectory.

He says he was always interested in the end game: *How do we know we are successful?* He believes in metrics, but adds,

> If you believe in the state test, that guides all your work—your hires, your professional development. But if you are measuring whether students are fulfilled as young people and they are working toward being strong community members, then you measure something else. Do the students have 21st century skills of collaboration? Do they have a strong community ethic?

The school's mission statement goal, "Creative and competent community leaders," matches the tagline of the district's mission: "*Community Schools, Thriving Students.*"

Mr. Hong says that the metrics for a physically and emotionally safe school environment were his first priority. Then he wanted to "get the right people on the bus" by choosing staff for every position in the school who affirm each other and maintain a positive stance even in the face of challenges, who assume best intentions toward and from their colleagues, who can resolve conflicts, and who believe deeply that all students can be successful.

His staff exudes these attributes, and, as he said, "I interview each person myself and they have to be someone whose spirit is ready to take up this work. You pick the right people and you pay attention to how they feel. You must have adult fulfillment before you can as a group make changes for the whole school." He uses regular staff fulfillment surveys. Those metrics told him loud and clear that having 150+ students each day in short class periods was not good for teaching and learning or for adults trying to know their students and families well. He said, "We put our heads together with teachers and we decided on a completely different schedule."

As a result, each teacher has a total of 75 students in three block periods. The school devotes 80 minutes every other day to adult planning along with a 40-minute lunch. On Monday mornings, teachers have a longer first period so they can call or email parents to tell them how the young people are doing. The school uses the translation service Language Link to facilitate contact with parents whose first language is not English. The advisory periods once a day are a ratio of 19:1. He reports, "We built enthusiasm for the block schedule before we changed; we made sure we had materials for that type of schedule, and we knew from surveys that 95 percent of the staff were looking forward to this . . . we did not have to sell it. We made the change when people were behind it."

Secondly, Mr. Hong indicates that as the school moves toward stronger shared leadership perspective that includes youth development and youth leadership, he notices a different perspective among the adults. He said, "they say things like—I didn't know that middle school students were as thoughtful and capable as they are . . . they are not entities to be controlled. We are not doing school to them and not even for them. We are doing education with them." In this school, the following practices ensure that students are community-ready citizens and support student leadership and personal growth:

- Every student has a school job that helps the school community, and each student must participate in two social actions in the community.
- Every student presents five project-based learning presentations/ exhibitions each year; the projects build capacity to conduct research and solve community issues with this question in mind: How can I make the world around me a better place for everyone?

Mr. Hong says that previously he had an uninformed sense of parent participation or family engagement. Even though community mapping was a part of his preparation program, he thought that having a community school just meant providing services to students and families. He said,

Now I look at that view as patronizing and patriarchal. Through my work as community organizer, I see how we need to co-construct. I had to do self-work; they may not speak the same language I speak, but they have the knowledge and experience of another sort to be partners in this work. I don't even like to think of it as engagement, but of family partnerships.

His ability to interrogate his own work matches his deeper understanding of the CLE axioms: "Hopes and change are built on assets and dreams of locals and their communities" and "the people closest to the issues are best situated to discover answers to local concerns." As a result, Mr. Hong is now working on the school's wider image in the whole neighborhood because he does not hear good things in the larger community about the school.

He has secured a professional public relations person as a mentor, handed out a card with his cell phone to all parents at back-to-school night, and is working with his feeder schools and the neighborhood high school to cohere the schools for the benefit of students and families.

Like the School One principal, overlap between the day school and after-school is vital. The community school manager (also known in other chapters as a community school coordinator or director) and executive director of the community-based organization (CBO) sit on the leadership team, and the CBO staff attend the school's professional learning opportunities. As indicated in a report by the Center for Popular Democracy[11] on the Roosevelt community school story, the manager participates on a team that has addressed chronic absenteeism and suspension rates and reduced them significantly through targeted support systems on a Coordination of Services Team (COST).

The principal put aside money for a rainy-day fund—in one school year, he used this to retain two full-time employees when the enrollment, and the budget, were lower than anticipated. The school is applying for a local grant that requires demonstrated success before applying. The school is focused on adult fulfillment that in turn makes a difference for student outcomes. The school is now moving to understand what internal formative assessments will work for diagnosis and careful tracking of student progress.[12]

Principal Hong is clear that culture and climate precede emphasis on academics. This is contrary to the typical demands that a principal be an instructional leader in such prescribed ways as number of visits to classrooms each week or a focus on math or reading. He redefines instructional leadership as putting key abstract resources in place so that, when teachers make joint decisions about curricular and instructional approaches and emphases, they stick to them. Because of that, the move to personalized learning came about only after the adults had the foundation of time and people resources so essential to doing hard work on behalf of children. Principal Hong said,

I know that most people in central office were concerned that I was not spending as much time on instruction. Instinctually, I thought it would be a mistake trying to get teachers to be technically better. For me it was about culture; it was always culture before program (instruction). When I first came here, it was probably about 80–20 with the bulk of my time on operations, organizational management and culture. Over time that has balanced to about 40–60 with the larger piece being instruction. Right balance . . . 70–30 . . . I would never had been able to get there if I had focused on the test score metric. But I was always going to stay here for many years; I wasn't on my way anywhere else. I knew that ten years minimum would be my goal to take this school from possible to good to great.

Principal Hong was honored by the district as a strong and successful leader, and his school is making progress on the metrics he thinks are key. While academic metrics are important measures of school success, Principal Hong is finely attuned to school climate and the social-emotional needs of students as well.

As we walked out of the school, a student came up to him and said, "Mr. Hong, somebody just called me a swami. I'm not sure what that is but it wasn't nice." He asked the student some questions about who and how, and he told the student he would look into it and see what that was about. So, there is always work to do on emotional safety in a middle school, but the right people in the right place with the right leader makes any visitor think they are on the right path. However, identifying the appropriate response to a complex issue is not something you can just bottle up and replicate.

CRITERIA AND AXIOMS COME ALIVE IN COMMUNITY SCHOOLS

If you want to build a ship, don't recruit the men to gather the wood, divide the work and give orders. Instead, teach them to yearn for the vast and endless sea.

—Antoine de Saint-Exupery

In this section, we talk about how the two leaders and their schools exemplify the key criteria of community and axioms of the Community

Learning Exchange. The shared characteristic of reciprocity is in evidence throughout, but the specifics of how the leaders and the schools live and breathe the criteria and axioms we make transparent.

Today's school leaders are given improvement targets (e.g., test scores, attendance, and suspensions) without much time or resources. A natural reaction is to take immediate action—do something quickly, a quick fix to ameliorate a problem. While these principals accept the urgency of school improvement, they embark on processes that ensure long-term impacts where all constituents are empowered. The principals rely on their communities (in and out of schools) to be community school entrepreneurs. Both use inquiry (ask questions to all community members) and action (engage in strategies).

A number of characteristics from the criteria for successful community schools and Community Learning Exchange axioms (see table 2.1) illustrate what this work looks like. Both principals have an equity-driven passion to ensure "all means all." To achieve this, the principals seek ideas and enact strategies for the specific populations of students in their schools. Both engage in shared leadership within their schools. Both fully link the school day to after-school.

Like other successful community school leaders, they use data to inform what works. However, they choose data sources that actually move the work forward; at the outset, they had to resist using the standard sets of data as the sole source of improvement metrics. Their leadership actions, while risky in some districts, paid off in the end. In our current data-driven educational landscape, the principals are clear-eyed about what the important data include: intuition, anecdotes, growth, reflection, fulfillment, dialogue, and cultural context, as well as standardized tests. Data-driven leaders use data that are useful to different constituencies.

In the end, the principals are leaders who understand leadership is a dynamic process, not an act of a sole person who makes broad, sweeping changes. The leaders cross-traditional boundaries in school (e.g., sharing leadership among teachers/staff and administration as well as with community school coordinators and the CBO) and in the community (e.g., honored and utilized the expertise of community members). The leaders are culturally responsive because they have their eyes on larger structural responses that reinforce equity and excellence, including providing wraparound services for their schools, engaging multiple persons in collaborative leadership, and re-imagining school curricular and instructional responses.

The two courageous principals epitomize the best in leaders of today and tomorrow. They talk and walk engaging practices and do not portend to have all the answers. The principals put their principles on the line. They do not need to be convinced of the philosophical "why" of being equity-minded leaders, but they did have to think through *how* to put equity-focused leadership preparation into action. Their ability to embody what Freire (1970) calls praxis (reflection and action) stands out in these tales. They focus on the procedural *how* to engage with others to do the work for all, trusting their moral compasses and marshaling evidence and resources (abstract and money) to support their directions.[13]

We are often asked, "What does the Community Learning Exchange work look like in schools?" Principals Agustín and Hong provide us with vivid accounts of what this work looks like in action. These principals engage their schools in enacting Community Learning Exchange axioms in order to meet the successful criteria for leading a community school.

FINAL THOUGHTS

We began this research journey to understand and to learn from those doing the work of community schools and from those who embrace and live the tenets of Community Learning Exchanges. Our summary learning provides a foil for what this work looks like for community school leaders:

1. Pay attention to your own intuition, experience, and knowledge. Remember that data reflect the plural—use multiple metrics to ascertain affective and cognitive growth.
2. Ensure time for building and sustaining relational trust and effective collaboration of teachers, community school personnel, and staff in your school and parents and community members outside of the school.
3. Look at structures, particularly how student and teacher time is used. How does time use align with the school's values? Time is one of the key resources, yet we tend to keep the old models in place as if they were sacrosanct without innovating or re-imagining. How can you re-imagine instructional minute use, for example?

4. Recognize and celebrate. Be relentless with acknowledging the assets in your school and community.
5. Be entrepreneurial in the best sense of the word—innovative, risk-taking, tactical, groundbreaking; look for additional resources (people, time, and money) and tell the story of your school to wider audiences.
6. Think of leadership as a collaborative function. Utilize the positional power of the school leader to invite and empower the community to engage in important decisions.
7. Be courageous! Lead and model what it looks like to understand the context of your community, *the power of place* and engage with, not for, community members, *the wisdom of people*.

Our hope was to bring to life how to enact community schools with axioms from the Community Learning Exchange philosophy and practices as guiding lights. In these tales, we see authentic, practical, doable inquiry and actions that lead to empowered, equity-driven outcomes for leaders, teachers, students, parents, and community members. Our quest began with seeking ideas from those doing the work. We, like the two principals, live the ultimate axiom that the answers to our most pressing problems reside in the wisdom of those doing the work addressing the circumstances we want to alter.

Our challenge to you, the readers, is not to use this as a step-by-step guide. Instead, we challenge you to engage with your community to find the strategies and actions that are right for you and your community. To be imagineers. That is where you will find your answer—in local decision making that is fundamentally different because of the relationships and creativity of those who gather in schools and communities to imagine what success looks like for all our students and how that can be achieved.

REFERENCES

Dewey, J. (1938). *Experience & education.* New York: Touchstone.
Dryfoos, J., & Maguire, S. (2002). *Inside full-service community schools.* Thousand Oaks, CA: Corwin Press.
Dryfoos, J., Quinn, J., & Barkin, C. (2005), Eds. *Community schools in action: Lessons from a decade of practice.* New York: Oxford University Press.

Epstein, J. L., Sanders, M. G., & Simon, S. (2008). *School, family and community partnerships: Your handbook for action.* Thousand Oaks, CA: Corwin Press.

Freire, P. (1970). *The pedagogy of the oppressed.* New York: The Continuum Publishing Co.

Grubb, N. (2009). *The money myth.* New York: Routledge.

Grubb, N., & Tredway, L. (2010). *Leading from the inside out: Expanded roles for teachers in equitable schools.* Boulder, CO: Paradigm Publishers.

Guajardo, M., Guajardo, F., Janson, C., & Militello, M. (2016). *Reframing community partnerships in education: Uniting the power of place and wisdom of people.* New York: Routledge.

Henderson, A. T., Mapp, K. L., Johnson, V. R., & Davies, D. (2007). *Beyond the bake sale: The essential guide to family-school partnerships.* New York: The New Press.

Jacobson, R., Hodges, R., & Blank, M. (2011). Mutual support: The community school strategy. *Principal Leadership, 12*(2), 18–22.

Militello, M., & Heffernan, N. (2009). Which one is "just right"? What educators should know about formative assessment systems. *International Journal of Educational Leadership Preparation, 4*(3), 1–8.

Militello, M., Sireci, S., & Schweid, J. (2008, March). *Intent, purpose, and fit: An examination of formative assessment systems in school districts.* Paper presented at the American Educational Research Association, New York, NY.

Nachmanovitch, S. (1993). *Free play: Improvisation in life and art.* New York: Tarcher/Putnam.

Safir, Shane. (2017). *The listening leader: Creating the conditions for an equitable school transformation.* San Francisco: Jossey-Bass.

Spillane, J. (2006). *Distributed leadership.* San Francisco: Jossey-Bass.

Spillane, J., & Coldren, A. (2011). *Diagnosis and design for school improvement.* New York: Teachers College Press.

Chapter Three

Community School Teacher Leaders Enhance Learning

Ellen Pais, Sarah Hurst, Deborah Lowe, Jennifer Rosenbaum, and Jessica Wadle

Imagine a school where teachers are empowered to take charge of students' academic needs and make students' well-being front and center of all school decisions. Imagine a school that makes equity a priority and ensures students, educators, families, and staff thrive because their holistic needs are met through programs and services held on-site. Imagine what happens when teachers are leading transformative changes that impact all aspects of the school community. Imagine what happens when structures are in place to support the developmental needs of the whole child. This chapter brings these imaginings to life, and describes one school's transformative journey.

EMBRACING A WHOLE CHILD EDUCATION PHILOSOPHY THROUGH COMMUNITY SCHOOLS

A community school is a place and a strategy grounded in the belief that all children can achieve regardless of their circumstances. This philosophy prioritizes students' academic needs and well-being. The school is also a place where students, educators, families, and staff thrive because their holistic needs are met. Embedded within a community school are the supports provided by district staff, local government agencies, and community members to fulfill a vision of meeting the needs of the whole child.

In these schools, after-school programs, health services, adult education, teacher wellness, and food pantries provide resources for children and families. Community schools are deeply connected to the uniqueness of their community and respond to local issues and political and policy changes—in crisis and in joy.

Teachers play an essential leadership role in creating a successful community school. Teachers know their students' strengths and needs, they know families, and they understand how schools operate. Getting their buy-in is critical; they often determine whether a strategy or program will work in a school and classroom. Instead of passive acquiesce to implementation of a strategy, teachers in community schools have a role in leadership and decision making.

It's hard to imagine anyone in a school who understands the challenges our country's students are facing better than teachers—especially in areas of high poverty. Teachers know that students learn better when their basic needs are met because then teachers can focus on their core purpose free of distractions: teaching students to learn.

But too often, what happens outside of the classroom creates barriers to learning. In most schools, teachers accept these challenges and bravely move forward with their curriculum, working hard to make instruction meaningful, engaging, and impactful for all students. Teachers in high-poverty schools are often advised during their preservice training to keep breakfast bars or other snacks in their cabinets to feed hungry students, so that missing a meal doesn't turn into missing a lesson.

Teachers around the country are concerned about their students' well-being and want strategies to address barriers to learning. They don't see these barriers as excuses, but they understand that hunger, homelessness, trauma, and physical and mental health affect learning.

In 2015, Scholastic surveyed the state teachers of the year—the best teachers in each state. When asked what their funding priorities would be to meaningfully impact student learning, teachers' top choices were anti-poverty initiatives, early learning, and reducing barriers to learning, such as access to wraparound services and health care (Worrell, 2015). Quoting Maine's Teacher of the Year, the *Washington Post* wrote,

> "Those three factors in many ways are the white elephant in the living room for us in education," said Jennifer Dorman, Maine's 2015 Teacher of the Year who teaches special-education classes for seventh- and eighth-graders. "As teachers, we know those factors present huge barriers to our students' success. Helping students cope with those three factors is probably the most

important part of my job. But on a national-level, those problems are not being recognized as the primary obstacles."

A nationally representative survey of 4,721 public school educators (principals and teachers) in 2016 found that educators overwhelmingly agreed with the statement "Many of my students face barriers to learning from outside of the school environment." Ninety-eight percent of educators in high-poverty schools agreed with that statement, as did two-thirds of teachers in low-poverty schools (Scholastic, n.d.). Teachers are telling us that these barriers impact student learning, but too often policy makers, education reformers, and others ignore the realities our children and teachers face daily.

Both teachers' unions, the American Federation of Teachers and the National Education Association, are advocates for community schools as a strategy to achieve whole child education. The unions promote the role of teachers in community schools as a national priority, as well as the collaboration between teachers and principals that is essential to meeting the instructional and support needs of students in a well-functioning community school.

What happens inside and outside the classroom matters, and teachers need help removing barriers to learning and creating powerful learning partnerships. Community schools offer teachers that support by providing wraparound services that remove barriers to learning and by enhancing learning opportunities to meet a student's academic, social-emotional, and developmental needs.

HAAT: A TEACHER-LED COMMUNITY SCHOOL

A distinction that HAAT holds for me is that we (staff, teachers, parents, and community partners) subscribe to a common vision: to provide students a sense of belonging and to give them multiple opportunities to develop a sense of purpose and direction.

—Marc Nord, Counselor

This chapter explores the roles of teachers in a community school, Humanitas Academy of Art and Technology, known as HAAT, a teacher-led pilot school on the Esteban E. Torres High School campus in East Los Angeles. In this school, teachers take on additional leadership roles that aren't typical in most public and public charter schools, making it a strong illustration of the power of teacher leadership in community schools.

HAAT is one of five separate pilot high schools at Torres High School, the first new high school campus built in East Los Angeles in 80 years to relieve persistent overcrowding at nearby schools. Torres High was constructed to house five independent small schools on one campus. HAAT, one of the five small schools, opened in 2010 as a result of the Public School Choice process in the Los Angeles Unified School District (LAUSD). The intent of LAUSD's process was "to improve school performance and increase student achievement through innovative, efficient, and rigorous school plans" (Los Angeles Unified School District, n.d.).

Public School Choice (2009 to 2013) enabled teacher-led design teams, nonprofits, and charter school operators to submit plans to assume responsibility for newly built schools and chronically underperforming schools. In the 2009–2010 Public School Choice competition, teacher-led design groups advised by Los Angeles Education Partnership won the opportunity to launch all five new small schools on the Torres campus.

In LAUSD, pilot schools are public schools that use standard district enrollment procedures but have autonomy over budget, staffing, governance, school calendar, and curriculum and assessment. Each pilot school on the Torres campus has its own career theme and is run as a completely autonomous small community school. The five small schools collaborate by sharing space, an athletics program, school dances, and a community school coordinator. The coordinator, an employee of Los Angeles Education Partnership, began working on campus in 2010, the year the schools opened.

In the 2017–2018 school year, HAAT's population was almost exclusively Latino (98.5 percent) and had a free and reduced-price lunch rate of 92.6 percent.[1] HAAT has been succeeding. The school's four-year cohort graduation rate increased 21 percent points from 73.9 percent in 2013 to 94.5 percent in 2016—compared to 77.3 percent in LAUSD overall (CDE, Dataquest). According to the principal of HAAT, 41 percent of graduates in the class of 2016 enrolled in a four-year university. This statistic compares favorably to the 44 percent of the class of 2015 nationally that enrolled in a four-year college.[2]

Also, on California's Smarter Balanced tests given to 11th graders, HAAT juniors have made noteworthy progress in math and English competency. The percentage of HAAT students who did not meet standards decreased by double digits from 2015 to 2017: 20 percentage points in English language arts and 29 percentage points in math.[3]

How have teachers helped make HAAT a successful community school? We turn to their role next.

TEACHERS' ROLE IN COMMUNITY SCHOOLS

> At HAAT, we thrive on collaboration. It's never boring and never lonely. Teachers work side by side to develop dynamic, culturally relevant curriculum and have the resources we need to make magic happen. Students are encouraged to use their voice and take learning beyond the classroom. HAAT is more than a high school—it's a creative community that we get to build together.
>
> —Adriana Yugovich, Art Teacher

In a community school, teachers do more than teach classes, and they do more than refer students to external student supports. In HAAT, teachers strategically align everything with the school's mission and values, from instruction, to social-emotional learning, to college access. To accomplish this, trusting relationships are essential. The school culture intentionally promotes and nurtures trusting relationships for the well-being of students and educators.

Teachers are advocates for their students; they build relationships and help students blossom. They lead the charge for academic rigor and students' mastery of content. Teachers promote student self-efficacy by embedding life skills, relevance, student leadership, goal setting, and student self-reflection into classrooms and across the school. As leaders, teachers put themselves on the front lines of issues affecting parents including school climate and relationships.

In this section, we describe the ways in which teachers in a community school build trusting relationships, participate in governance and decision making, use integrated student supports, and help create a school climate that lessens trauma and promotes well-being. Most important,

HAAT provides examples of how teachers work hand-in-hand with the community school coordinator to make meaningful opportunities.

Trust and Collaboration

Community schools build an environment that nurtures and supports trusting relationships that lay the foundation for quality instruction, social-emotional support, parent and community engagement, and school leadership. At HAAT, teachers prioritize knowing their students' strengths and needs in order to best support them. For teachers, this starts with relationships: with each other, with students, with parents, and with the community.

HAAT embodies teamwork at its best. The staff understand that collaboration is essential for achieving more with limited resources. Unlike large, traditional schools where educators often operate in silos and may lack connections to outside resources, HAAT's community school staff recognize collaboration and partnerships as indispensable for student success because they can't meet students' needs alone. When a student needs food or mental health services, for example, HAAT teachers know the community school coordinator has a partner organization that can help. Partnership and collaboration build trust that transforms school culture.

Community schools use collaborative strategies that build relationships and promote teacher efficacy. Teachers who embrace collaboration are well suited for the structure of a community school. This type of approach is validated by research that demonstrates that prioritizing trusting relationships and collaboration between adults at a school is well-placed (Ronfeldt, Farmer, McQueen, & Grissom, 2015; Herman, Dawson, Dee, Greene, Maynard, Redding, & Darwin, 2008; Waldron & McLeskey, 2010; Jones & Shindler, 2016).

At HAAT, teachers are trained in the work of Michael Fullan's "right drivers," Richard DuFour's professional learning communities, and Pedro Noguera's focus on equity, as well as models for school improvement, such as Cognitive Coaching and Adaptive Schools. Each of these models contributes to the five essential supports for an effective urban school learning environment: school leadership, parent and community ties, professional capacity of the faculty, a student-centered learning climate, and a coherent instructional plan (Bryk, Sebring, Allensworth, Easton, & Luppescu, 2010).

Tony Bryk and his colleagues maintained in their highly regarded study of Chicago Public Schools that these five essential supports promote a culture of trusting relationships and reflective conversations, which are the cornerstone of high-functioning schools. At a community school, these conversations build teachers' capacity to problem-solve and engage in meaningful dialogue.

At HAAT, reflective conversations happen in meetings of the Instructional Leadership Team, faculty, departments, and the Coordination of Services Team. Educators have ongoing conversations and engage in joint problem-solving to address issues of attendance, behavior, and academic performance. Trusting relationships among teachers and administrators enable them to confront conflicts and challenges in order to find solutions.

Governance and Decision Making

At a community school, leadership and ownership of decision making is very different. When asked to describe her role at HAAT, Principal Deborah Lowe responded, "Ask the teachers: who is in charge? They respond, they are! Ask the students: who is in charge? They respond, they are! And they are both right. That is what a community school looks like!"

In many schools, the hierarchical structure for decision making, delegating tasks, and demanding conformity to someone else's agenda often makes progress difficult because they are not personally invested in the outcome. In community schools, the principal fosters a collaborative, school-wide climate and culture, trusts teachers to build students' academic proficiency, and encourages the community school coordinator's leadership of the community school strategy. Distributed leadership and collaborative decision making that build school staff members' sense of worth and self-efficacy leads to school improvement, teacher satisfaction, and better student outcomes (Prilleltensky, Neff, & Bessell, 2016; Papay & Kraft, 2017; Quintero, 2017; McCarthy & Rubinstein, 2017).

The governance of a community school is supported by a problem-solving process that encourages teachers to look at data, engage with partners, and develop collaborative solutions. The teachers and partners then implement solutions and use updated data to reflect upon the process and impact. For example, to address behavior issues at HAAT, teachers and administrators consider both quantitative data (e.g., attendance, academic performance, mental health referrals, and discipline) and qualitative data (e.g., survey data from teachers, students and parents, and input from the community school coordinator).

From the start, HAAT school leaders recognized that to have the quality of relationships they desired, they needed to address the underlying causes of behavior, not ignore them. School leaders needed a strategy for complicated conversations between students and teachers and explored critical events and feelings appropriately. HAAT brought in a partner, the California Conference for Equality and Justice, to train educators in restorative justice. Faculty regularly reflected on the strategies to ensure that everyone used a respectful approach to de-escalation of disagreements and problem-solving.

The school also created a staff position for a restorative justice counselor. Now, the communication strategies are embedded in the fabric of the school as policy and practice, even for resolving disagreements between staff members, leading to stronger relationships throughout the school. The suspension rate at HAAT dropped from 1.7 percent in 2014–2015 to zero in 2016–2017, and it received the highest performance level possible on the California School Dashboard for this indicator.

The community school coordinator can help teachers solve a complex problem or issue by listening to the concerns of teachers and partners and helping them create and implement strategies. An example of this integrated approach is the delivery of college and career readiness at HAAT. Teachers were confronted with a problem: the school had a limited number of counselors, but HAAT wanted all students prepared for college. One teacher took a leadership role to overcome this challenge. She became very involved with Los Angeles Education Partnership to learn college-access strategies that teachers could implement. She shared these with her fellow teachers, who jointly found ways to include these strategies in instruction.

Teachers embedded résumé writing, college essays, and preparation of applications into the school day. To support the teachers, the coordinator and school counselors arranged training for advisory teachers and identified college-access partners and volunteers. The coordinator organized workshops on the Free Application for Federal Student Aid, drop-in centers for students to prepare applications, as well as mock interviews and career days. Together, the teachers, counselors, community school coordinator and partners created a system to ensure that all students, including immigrant students covered under the Deferred Action for Childhood Arrivals program, receive college and career support.

Integrated Student Supports

Public school teachers often identify needs that students have, but do not know about appropriate resources or have a process to connect students with these resources. In a community school, there is a structure for helping teachers connect students to assistance.

In a high-functioning community school like HAAT, teacher teams meet regularly in faculty meetings by grade level and department to review individual student progress. The school has a protocol for looking at risk factors, as well as academic growth. The community school coordinator attends these meetings and then arranges for resources to meet students' needs.

For example, HAAT teachers identified twins with low attendance and contacted the Pupil Services and Attendance (PSA) counselor. The PSA counselor investigated and discovered that the twins' mother had cancer. The PSA counselor then referred the twins for mental health counseling and to the school's weekly on-campus food pantry—both organized by the community school coordinator.

The twins' attendance improved since they did not have to spend part of their school day seeking food from off-campus sources. HAAT teachers also identified an upsurge in girl violence in ninth grade. The community school coordinator invited a local nonprofit that builds social skills to work with ninth-grade girls whose truancy and violent behaviors indicated they had likely experienced trauma.

In another example, teachers at HAAT and the other schools on the Torres High campus recognized that a very high number of students were experiencing mental health episodes. The existing mental health resource at the campus was inadequate, and these mental health episodes became more frequent and more extreme. Consequently, the community school coordinator organized five mental health providers to supplement the district resources, and the number of episodes dropped 90 percent, according to the school counselor.

This process of recognizing a fundamental need and securing resources happens repeatedly at HAAT. In Coordination of Services Team meetings, teachers identify students who need mental health counseling, glasses, or food. The school has the resources to meet these needs—or the community school coordinator to locate the right resource—because it is a community school.

Building robust school and community partnerships to provide essential student services, such as after-school programming, college-access resources, mental health or health care, is hard work, generally done by the community school coordinator. However, the coordinator depends on clear lines of communication with teachers that can identify their students' needs. The coordinator ensures that HAAT has integrated supports to address students' nonacademic needs so that teachers' number one priority remains instruction.

School Climate and Trauma

The quality of school climate can change based on the well-being of students and staff. Particularly in low-income schools, many students have experienced multiple adverse childhood experiences, known as ACES. These include abuse, neglect, witnessing domestic violence, substance abuse in the home, and other traumatizing experiences. A landmark study by Kaiser Permanente and the Centers for Disease Control and Prevention demonstrated that adverse childhood experiences were associated with social dysfunction, substance abuse, and chronic illnesses (Felitti, Anda, Nordenberg, Williamson, Spitz, Edwards, Koss, & Marks, 1998).

Children who have experienced multiple adverse childhood experiences are more likely to have academic and social-emotional problems at school. Many schools punish this behavior, however, educators are increasingly responding to these behaviors with the kind of whole child approach that is found in community schools. This includes more inclusive instructional strategies, positive behavior supports, multi-tiered systems of support that link students with services, and restorative justice.

In addition to HAAT's significant investment in restorative justice, the school partnered with its after-school provider, EduCare, on a pilot project about ACEs and integrating social-emotional learning into the curriculum. EduCare selected HAAT because the pilot project was well-aligned with the school's philosophy. In the project, students received assistance that addressed their traumatic experiences and teachers learned strategies to support students.

Teachers in high-functioning community schools also ensure that the school climate and instructional pedagogy are student-centered. Teachers work to connect with their students in many ways, such as considering students' backgrounds as valuable resources to enrich the curriculum. At every grade level, teachers emphasize the importance of student leadership skills, student voice, active participation, and self-advocacy. Teachers get to know their students through authentic instructional experiences.

Some schools employ data-gathering tools, such as the 40 Developmental Assets or Healthy Kids Survey, to learn more about their students as individuals and as a group and then create strategies, with teachers and partners, to increase students' protective factors and assets. Examples of such activities include book clubs, mentorship programs, and community service.

Priorities and Competencies for Teachers in Community Schools

Community school teachers are equipped to deliver student-centered and student-empowered instruction. This means minimization of direct instruction, work sheets, and rote memorization and an increase in activities that promote critical thinking, communication, and creativity. In a community school classroom, teachers often arrange desks to encourage group conversations, rather than facing forward for a more traditional lecture by a teacher. The quality of a classroom is measured by the hum of students working together to understand a scientific or historical theory rather than the quiet of a pin-drop.

Teachers deliver information with an emphasis on local context and cultural relevance. Teachers ask students to make real-world connections that stem from their own experiences, not textbooks describing places that have no relationship to the community. Class time is an opportunity for both teachers and students to learn, because teachers encourage students to share their viewpoints and conceptual understanding.

Teachers Connect Students to the Community

In a community school, the neighborhood is the connection to real-life learning. Teachers bring the community into the classroom by creating lessons that partner with local professionals, such as an architect or

grocery-store owner, which makes learning relevant and much more interesting to students. For example, generating a project with the local transit
agency gives students the chance to learn in a local context.

This level of commitment to authentic learning requires the teacher and
the coordinator to know the neighborhood and to connect to its business,
government, and arts assets. In addition, bringing a local artist or business
leader into the classroom who shares the same roots as the students helps
them envision a future for themselves. For these efforts to be successful,
teachers and partners need to establish clear expectations and roles.

For example, the HAAT digital media teacher received a grant to collaborate with Working Assumptions, a California-based nonprofit, to create a curricular unit integrated into the advanced digital imaging class for
seniors. The students photographed the push and pull of work and family
they saw in their lives. The assignment culminated in the "Home/Work"
photography exhibit at the Armory Center for the Arts, curated and mar-
keted by students.

Teachers Promote Service and Engagement

Teachers in community schools encourage student service and community
engagement. When a school participates in activities that benefit the community, students and families see that the school is connected to the community. Community school teachers promote character and civic investment as
life skills and values. HAAT teachers develop these skills by working with
the coordinator to create lessons that promote civic engagement.

For example, HAAT has organized voter registration and blood drives
and HAAT students join in the operation of the weekly on-campus food
pantry. HAAT teachers also promote community engagement by integrating community data, such as health, employment, educational attainment,
home ownership, and availability of banks and grocery stores, into lessons
to motivate students to investigate their local area.

Teachers Use and Value Authentic Assessment

At a student-centered community school, teachers' assessment of student
performance should look different than at a traditional school. Traditional
schools will often use assessments such as multiple choice, fill-in-the-

blank, and true-false tests. In contrast, authentic assessments use a task, question, or open-ended challenge for a student to respond to, scored with a rubric. According to Jon Mueller, both approaches support a school's mission to develop productive students. But traditional assessments test the attainment of a body of knowledge and skills, while authentic assessment furthers student-centered learning by testing a student's ability to accomplish tasks that are useful in the real world (Mueller, 2018).

This distinction is important for a community school that connects to the community in which students live. HAAT uses Los Angeles Education Partnership's Humanitas instructional model, which "empowers students through project-based learning that encourages critical thinking, writing and verbal skills." Authentic assessment aligns with project-based learning and the application of knowledge.

An example of HAAT's use of interdisciplinary, project-based learning with authentic assessment is found in U.S. history for juniors. English, history, and art teachers collaborate on a study of the 1920s, including Prohibition. The speakeasy project is the culminating assessment, which community members attend. Students re-create a 1920s speakeasy and dress as historical characters. In character, they speak about the person and answer questions. Students are graded in part on how well they present this time period and their character. The speakeasy project has become an annual highlight of HAAT's school year.

Teachers Develop Students' Leadership Skills

Teachers promote leadership skills in the classroom and across the campus. In addition to encouraging students to actively participate in discussions, group projects, and project-based learning, faculty empower students to experience different roles to complete tasks. Community schools often employ peer-to-peer strategies to create a welcoming climate, mediate disputes, and encourage healthy behaviors. Teachers value students taking on these responsibilities and provide them with the skills and opportunities to be leaders.

HAAT holds school-wide mixed grade-level discussion circles to build community. Teachers recommend students to be trained as circle leaders, recruiting students who are not traditional leaders, but have the personality and potential to become strong leaders. These trained circle leaders go on to become leaders in their advisory periods and assist in delivering HAAT's transition program for incoming ninth graders.

Teachers Foster Student Ownership for Their Education

Teachers in a community school also encourage students' development of skills for postsecondary success by empowering them to take ownership of their educational careers. Portfolios that include a students' body of work over a school year enables students to see their progress and where they have struggled.

Also, in partnership with their teachers, students reflect on their academic and social-emotional path and plan for improvement and growth. Twice per year, HAAT has student-led conferences in which students—rather than teachers—take the lead in presenting their coursework and academic goals, as well as their strengths, assets, and challenges to parents. To prepare students, teachers integrate self-reflection into each course. With criteria from teachers, HAAT students assess their progress toward learning targets and provide evidence of their own learning. This approach has increased students' ability to advocate for themselves and to have meaningful conversations about their portfolio with parents.

Teachers Foster Parent Engagement

In community schools, parents are teachers' partners in educating children. Teachers in community schools encourage parents to share their observations and concerns and to participate in creating solutions. This requires an intentional strategy for building relationships between teachers and parents. Student-led conferences is one strategy that HAAT uses to increase parent engagement. Attendance by parents at student-led conferences is regularly more than 90 percent.

Also, this approach changes the typical conversations between students and their parents, and teachers and parents. The aforementioned Home/Work photography project, and other class projects that relate to the community, also increase parent engagement. As students photographed their families, homes, and work, parents and students gained an appreciation of the artistic value of their home life and parents began to see their children as artists.

FINAL THOUGHTS

Community school teachers understand the fundamental principles of a high-functioning community school that provides a quality education and comprehensive supports. These include:

Equity: Teachers in a community school acknowledge that the path to success is harder for some students than others. Equity means that each student gets the support they need to be successful. Teachers ensure each student is challenged and has the relevant instruction they need to achieve academically. The community school makes it possible for teachers to use a system of integrated supports, or multi-tiered systems of support, to refer the students for assistance. Community school teachers identify gaps and needs so that the coordinator and community can meet them.

Well-being: Teachers in community schools know how to prevent burnout and compassion fatigue in themselves as they help students burdened by childhood trauma. Fortunately, brain research and social science research are identifying effective ways for teachers to embrace these children while maintaining their own well-being and a positive school environment.

Restorative justice and positive behavior supports: In implementing smarter strategies to teach young people, especially those who come to school with trauma, teachers learn restorative practices that strengthen communication skills and solve problems rather than just smoothing out feelings. Teachers in community schools are prepared to develop deep, trusting relationships with their peers and students.

Community assets and wisdom: Teachers in community schools learn about the community in which they teach. They respect community assets and take a strengths-based approach to students, families, and partners. Teachers embed the assets of the community into their teaching and design project-based lessons that incorporate the community so that students relate what they learn to the world around them.

As we write this chapter, we understand that teaching is a very demanding career. The demands in the classroom, the needs of students, and the struggle to support the well-being of teachers are real challenges. But a collaborative climate and integrated supports like those in the HAAT community school help mitigate these challenges.

In HAAT, teachers deliver rigorous instruction linked to the real world and community. They support the holistic development of students. In teams, they monitor individual students' progress toward goals and ensure that students get the support they need.

Teaching in a community school like HAAT can be very fulfilling: belonging to a team that shares a common vision can reduce isolation and stress. A holistic, partnership-based approach like the one at HAAT means students' needs are being met so they are prepared to learn and teachers can focus on delivering quality instruction in the classroom. Community schools are great place for students to learn and for teachers to work. Just listen to what two HAAT students say:

> "The teachers at HAAT take the time to get to know you and ask you about your personal life. They get to know who you are, and they show you that they care. They get to know you and once they do that, they know how to work with you."
>
> —Gabriela, HAAT student

> "Our teachers support us in what we want to do and who we want to be. They look at what we are interested in and work it into our class. I really like my teachers and feel connected to them."
>
> —Leilani, HAAT student

The transformative power of community schools has been well documented in HAAT's teacher-led journey to create teacher-driven contexts for school redesign and student success. In its quest to focus on the needs of the whole child, HAAT embraced the collective wisdom of staff, students, and the community to make substantive modifications in school policy, practices, and services, resulting in life-changing outcomes for students and their families. HAAT's journey clearly underscores the sentiment that teachers know what to do, and when given the support and freedom to teach and to lead, amazing things happen.

REFERENCES

Bryk, A. S., Sebring, P. B., Allensworth, E., Easton, J. Q., & Luppescu, S. (2010). *Organizing schools for improvement lessons from Chicago.* Chicago: University of Chicago Press.

Felitti, V. J., Anda, R. F., Nordenberg, D., Williamson, D. F., Spitz, A. M., Edwards, V., Koss, M. P., & Marks, J. S. (1998). Relationship of childhood abuse and household dysfunction to many of the leading causes of death in adults: The Adverse Childhood Experiences (ACE) Study. *American Journal of Preventive Medicine, 14*(4), 245–258.

Herman, R., Dawson, P., Dee, T., Greene, J., Maynard, R., Redding, S., & Darwin, M. (2008). Turning around chronically low-performing schools: A practice guide (NCEE #2008-4020). Washington, D.C.: National Center for Education Evaluation and Regional Assistance, Institute of Education Sciences, U.S. Department of Education. Retrieved from http://ies.ed.gov/ncee/wwc/publications/practiceguides.

Jones, A., & Shindler, J. (2016). Exploring the school climate—Student achievement connection: Making sense of why the first precedes the second. *Educational Leadership and Administration: Teaching and Program Development, v27*, 35–51.

Los Angeles Unified School District. (n.d.) *Public school choice history.* Retrieved from https://achieve.lausd.net/Page/2596.

McCarthy, J. E., & Rubinstein, S. A. (2017). *National study on union-management partnerships and educator collaboration in US public schools* (Collaborative School Leadership Initiative Working Paper). Retrieved from https://www.cecweb.org/wp-content/uploads/2017/10/Union_Management_Partnerships.pdf.

Mueller, J. (2018). *Authentic assessment toolbox.* Retrieved from http://jfmueller.faculty.noctrl.edu/toolbox/whatisit.htm.

Papay, J., & Kraft, M. (2017). Developing workplaces where teachers stay, improve, and succeed: Recent evidence on the importance of school climate for teacher success. In E. Quintero (Ed.), *Teaching in context: The social side of education reform.* Cambridge, MA: Harvard Education Press.

Prilleltensky, I., Neff, M., & Bessell, A. (2016). Teacher stress: What it is, why it's important, how it can be alleviated. *Theory Into Practice, 55*(2), 1–14.

Quintero, E. (Ed.). (2017). *Teaching in context: The social side of education reform.* Cambridge, MA: Harvard Education Press.

Ronfeldt, M., Farmer, S., McQueen, K., & Grissom, J. (2015). Teacher collaboration in instructional teams and student achievement. *American Educational Research Journal, 52*(3), 475–514.

Scholastic. (n.d.). *Teacher & principal school report: Focus on literacy.* Retrieved from http://www.scholastic.com/teacherprincipalreport/Scholastic -Teacher-and-Principal-School-Report-Literacy.pdf.

Waldron, N., & McLeskey, J. (2010). Establishing a collaborative culture through comprehensive school reform. *Journal of Educational and Psychological Consultation, 20(*1), 58–74.

Worrell, G. (2015, May 19). We surveyed the 2015 State Teachers of the Year [Blog post]. Retrieved October 1, 2018, from http://edublog.scholastic.com /post/we-surveyed-2015-state-teachers-year#.

Chapter Four

Re-imagining Teacher Preparation

The Role of Community Schools

JoAnne Ferrara and Diane W. Gómez

Pre-service teachers are an untapped resource for community schools. However thus far, the role of pre-service teachers has been neglected in community school literature (Ferrara, Santiago, & Siry, 2008; Gómez, Ferrara, Santiago, Fanelli, & Taylor, 2012). Although their presence in community schools is often considered uncharted territory, when successfully integrated into the community school strategy, pre-service teachers have potential to transform how community schools are implemented.

This chapter describes the role pre-service teachers play in community schools. The authors highlight the benefits of embedding teacher preparation in community school settings. In addition to the resources offered through a university partnership, the authors champion the presence of pre-service teachers for building professional learning among community school partners.

Preparing teachers for the realities of the classroom is a daunting task. Regardless of the school setting, many newly minted teachers often struggle to effectively handle daily classroom responsibilities. In addition to the typical duties of mastering the curriculum and managing the classroom environment, novice teachers often are unprepared to face unexpected challenges of student diversity, high levels of poverty, and under-resourced schools.

Pre-service teachers are better served if their preparation programs addressed poverty, family and community assets, family engagement, and partnerships within the context of a community school setting. The comprehensive, integrated community-based approach described in this chapter should be the norm rather than the exception.

As the composition of public schools change, more children arrive at school with barriers to learning (Santiago, Ferrara, & Blank, 2008). These barriers often are the result of opportunity gaps existing in many neighborhoods across the country. Many communities considered immune to shifting demographics are now facing challenges once reserved for their urban counterparts. Thus, many students in urban, suburban, and other communities arrive at school with significant barriers to learning (e.g., poverty, residential mobility, English as a new language, and interrupted schooling) that impede their success (Bankston & Caldas, 2017).

Further multiplying these barriers are limited opportunities brought about by educational and societal inequities. The challenges of these changing demographics often require schools to take a comprehensive, integrated approach to meeting student needs (Bankston & Caldas, 2017; Ferrara, 2014).

In schools where students' developmental needs far exceed the resources available at the classroom-level, a shift must occur in the ways schools are organized to address underserved students. Such reorganization asks schools to become a hub of the community providing a network of partners, programs, and practices to improve student outcomes. Against this backdrop, school personnel acquire a new set of skills to expand their view of how schools operate and to deepen their knowledge about shifting demographics in changing communities.

As might be expected, getting ready to teach in high-need schools requires the preparation of teachers who engage in a holistic approach to education, understand students' worldview, and possess the skills to influence the difficulties students face.

PREPARING PRE-SERVICE TEACHERS
FOR HIGH-NEEDS SCHOOLS

It is no surprise that many school districts serving poor children have teachers ill-equipped for classroom diversity, and consequently experience high levels of teacher turnover. School districts cite high attrition rates of novice teachers entering the profession with limited exposure to economically and culturally/linguistically diverse classrooms and limited knowledge of successful strategies to meet student needs (Howard, 2010).

Learning to teach in underserved communities begs for a "specialized knowledge base" (Anderson & Stillman, 2011) grounded in cultural competence and an equity-oriented framework for social change.

School districts look to the expertise of schools of education to groom highly effective teaching cadres of future teachers to meet ever-evolving demands. In response to districts' requests, schools of education strive to prepare beginning teachers with a specialized knowledge tailored to working in high-needs schools. Teacher educators understand that negotiating life in high-poverty schools involves more than a sole focus on pedagogical skills; in fact, it demands that pre-service teachers recognize the inequalities often present in children's lives.

Hence, the goal of teacher education programs is to develop individuals with competencies and empathic views that all students possess assets and are capable of academic success. One way to foster pre-service teachers' requisite skills is to provide robust, high-yield clinical experiences throughout their preparation program.

Early clinical field experiences must emphasize a holistic, assets-based approach to working with students. When pre-service teachers encounter students whose lives are dissimilar to their own, well-designed field placements become the conduit for understanding the inter relationship between school performance and the quality of students' lives (Ferrara et al., 2008). With extended field placements in settings that embrace and celebrate the diversity of student experiences, pre-service teachers develop both a broader perspective of student learning and a passion to enact culturally responsive practices. Community schools provide such opportunities for pre-service teachers.

Community schools, with their network of partnerships and mission to build an equitable education system for all students, provide authentic environments for the preparation of pre-service teachers. Given the spirit of collaboration and equity that is central to the community school strategy, it is no surprise that it aligns well with the Interstate Teacher Assessment and Support Consortium (InTASC) core teaching standards for teacher preparation (Council of Chief State School Officers, 2011).

After years of working alongside teacher candidates in community schools and observing their practice, we argue that community schools build a solid foundation for beginning teachers to become culturally competent and better able to understand a student's world and lived experiences.

Finding ways to fully immerse pre-service teachers in authentic experiences that challenge the status quo and foster equity is not an easy task. However, a university partnership designed as a professional development school (PDS) within the community school context permits pre-service teachers to live and experience a holistic approach to addressing students' needs.

Unlike university assisted community schools, which often take a lead partner agency role for implementation and oversight of the community school strategy, a PDS serves as an educational partner focused on innovation and ways to enhance teacher preparation, professional development, educational research, and student achievement. With its mission to impact school culture and practices, a PDS encourages pre-service teachers, in-service teachers, university faculty, and other community partners to work together to foster empathy, equity, and a rigorous curriculum centered on the needs of students and families.

Role of Pre-service Teachers in Community Schools

PDS partnerships can transform the culture of teaching, the nature of learning and expectations for collaboration in classrooms (Darling-Hammond, 1994). PDS partnerships with community schools provide the perfect arena to prepare pre-service teachers (Wepner, Gómez, Ferrara, 2013). Sharing ideas, practices, and conversations about teaching and learning creates a professional network of individuals (e.g., classroom teachers, social workers, parents, and health practitioners) responsible for raising the next generation of educators (Ferrara, 2014), as well as reducing teacher attrition and developing what Moir and colleagues (2009) call "the teacher quality gap."

The powerful cadre of on-site professionals at a community school can alter the way pre-service teachers think about and deliver instruction in 21st-century classrooms. Well beyond the notion that university students in the classroom are only an "extra pair of hands," pre-service teachers in community schools cultivate hope and inspiration among all school individuals that interact with them.

Community schools benefit from the activities pre-service teachers provide daily to meet student, and community needs, including classroom observations, tutoring, work with small groups, interactions with community-based organizations and parents, co-planning lessons with veteran teachers and college professors, and mostly importantly being part of networks of supports that embodies a community school.

Pre-service teachers become knowledgeable in the art of collaboration with their peers, colleagues, and partners. They apply a "whole child" philosophy. They serve as role models for students, representing the importance of education and that earning a university degree is a possibility. Over time, school practices and policies organically change to accommodate the needs and presence of pre-service teachers in the building.

To enact transformational practices in which all school members take an active role in the preparation of pre-service teachers requires strategic and thoughtful planning. The presence of pre-service teachers becomes the conduit for the leadership team to strategically plan coursework, field experiences, and projects to meet the needs of pre-service teachers as well as K–12 students, classroom teachers, partners, and school administrators. Therefore, the community school leadership team is essential. As one community partner indicated:

> Helping to coordinate the pre-service teachers' work with the parent group made me more aware of what they learned and didn't learn in their courses. The parents provided the student teachers with really powerful insights.

The primary function of the team, made up of representatives from all partnerships, is to identify the ways reciprocal benefits are provided for all stakeholders. Therefore, the leadership team is an integral part of the decision making for the types of activities taking place at the school to support the pre-service teachers in its buildings.

OUR MODEL: PDS AS COMMUNITY PARTNER

At Manhattanville College undergraduate pre-service teachers begin their community school experience during their first course in the Childhood Education program and the experience continues in each of the required courses throughout the program. Over the years of our partnership, we collected and analyzed data from pre-service teacher candidates' and veteran teachers' responses to a self-assessment dispositions checklist, journal reflections, informal surveys, and exit interviews.

Throughout the chapter, we provide a representative snapshot of recurring responses. Taken as a whole, these assignments provide a springboard for a closer examination of the impact pre-service teachers have in community schools and perceptions of their professional knowledge and their ability to work effectively with a range of learners.

Coursework is scaffolded to provide pre-service teachers with a framework to understand traditional and community schools. Throughout the program, opportunities for observation, tutoring, small group instruction, co-teaching, and reflective activities are embedded in the field component of the courses.

At various points during the program, course assignments require pre-service teachers to interact with the community school's partners, community school coordinator, teachers, parents, and the principal—all of the roles featured in this book. The interactions are designed to build capacity of pre-service teachers, in-service teachers, and partners. Moreover, the assignments create a space for all partners to actively participate in the preparation of teachers and to engage in what Zeichner (2010) called *boundary spanning*, the sharing of responsibilities across roles.

In addition, a series of integrative and comprehensive initiatives (e.g., on-site courses, field placement opportunities, internships, volunteer work, after-school employment, student teaching, and research projects) create school-wide connections that deepen the work and efficacy of veteran teachers and partners. The collaboration between pre-service teachers and community school partners is symbiotic and mutually beneficial.

Pre-service Teachers' Impact

Pre-service teachers are refreshing. As one administrator shared,

> I believe interns [pre-service teachers] breathe new life into the classroom, they are young, excited and have been exposed to new theories and instruction. When they share that with their cooperating teacher the results always benefit the school, classroom instruction, and ultimately the students. I also believe that the relationship between the interns and the cooperating teacher builds teacher efficacy in both the pre-service and the in-service teacher. (Principal #16, personal communication, 2017)

Their enthusiasm is contagious often reigniting veteran and in-service teachers' passion for the profession. As veteran teachers coach pre-service teachers, a context is created for learning *about* practice *in* practice (Ball & Cohen 1999, as cited in Darling-Hammond, 2006). Situating pre-service teachers in schools for the purpose of learning *about* practice *in* practice has the potential to build an interdependent, mutually beneficial culture. In this capacity, pre-service teachers become a catalyst for expanding veteran teachers' role beyond classroom engagement with partners to include the preparation of novice teachers. This new role for veterans facilitates a shift in professional identities.

Two veteran teachers commented:

I love the enthusiasm our interns bring to the building. It helps me remember my first year of teaching.

As a cooperating teacher working with a new group of student teachers each semester I improve my practice. I find myself more reflective because I want to provide the rationale for my decision-making.

At times the veteran teachers become the students. One principal reported, pre-service teachers "keep our faculty and staff up to speed on the latest and greatest technology" (Principal #1, five personal communications, 2017). While pre-service teachers bring new ideas grounded in theory into the classroom, they rely upon their mentor teachers to translate them into practice. In doing so, veteran teachers call upon their repertoire of strategies and years of experience to facilitate pre-service teachers' development while simultaneously enriching their own practice.

According to one principal, having pre-service teachers in her building makes "practitioners more reflective and puts us in touch with the latest research" (Principal #6, personal communication, 2017). At the same time, pre-service teachers are exposed to the practice of a whole child philosophy and the collaboration of a network of partners.

Community Partners

Interactions between partners and pre-service teachers provide reciprocal benefits. Pre-service teachers expand partners' skill set and knowledge base while partners help pre-service teachers understand what it looks like to work in collaboration. As they interact with community partners in the building, pre-service teachers increase partners' capacity to work with educators. One such example is our Shadow Project. For one day, pre-service teachers shadow community partners in their daily activities and interview them about the services they offer to the community school. This is an eye-opening experience for pre-service teachers. According to one pre-service teacher,

> I learned I enjoy being part of a collaborative team and can't do everything by myself. Since this school has a relationship with all the partners it allows the children for more support academically, socially, and emotionally.

Beyond the academic concerns, pre-service teachers become aware of the lived circumstances of the students, including the economic and social disparities that exist as well as the serious chronic health conditions often impacting student learning. Pre-service teachers immortalize the community school mission.

The Shadow Project provides a context for partners to broaden their perspective about education and the workings of a community school. As they share their role with pre-service teachers, partners reflect upon their practice, explain their agency's protocols, and respond to pre-service teachers' interview questions. In doing so, partners begin to view the inclusion of pre-service teachers as a responsibility to contribute to society by supporting teachers who develop a more collaborative approach.

Through these efforts, partners develop a "desire to be a part of the future teachers in our society" (Administrator #13, 2017). With this responsibility in mind, partners strive to support the development of a cadre of future teachers that recognize the needs of students and families. As one partner, a social worker reflected,

> Working with pre-service teachers introduced me to the field of teacher preparation. I became more aware of their limited knowledge of my field, so I made explicit connections for them. I altered my practice to provide support to pre-service teachers in our building. (personal communication, 2017)

More pre-service opportunities such as these would help train the types of teachers our schools need.

Families

When pre-service teachers "live" in a community school environment, their repertoire of experiences broaden. Often the exposure to families who represent cultures and languages other than their own encourages novice teachers to understand cultural norms and challenges their beliefs about diversity and poverty. Through interactions with families, pre-service teachers easily tap into the assets families bring to the table. Candidates view families as unbridled resources in their children's education.

The same can be said when families interact with pre-service teachers. Families begin to see pre-service candidates as assets and resources to navigate the school system and help their children achieve academically and socially.

Regardless of their position in the school, whether as a student teacher or serving as tutor or counselor in after-school programs, the presence of teacher candidates benefit the students, and in some instances, the entire family (Assistant Principal #3, personal communication, 2017). They also serve as role models and advocates.

Advocacy

We believe that to foster advocacy among future teachers requires an intentionality on behalf of teacher preparation programs. Over the years we witnessed student teachers become ambassadors for community schools. These novice teachers are deeply committed to schools that serve needs of the whole child through partnership networks. Student teachers routinely tell the public about the community school strategy and fiercely advocate for all schools to embrace the community school philosophy. As one pre-service teacher reflected:

> I . . . look at what the child's need is. I try to understand why there is a developmental delay and investigate what the community school can do to support it. I can't imagine what teachers do if they are not in a school like ours.

Our pre-service teachers serve as experts and liaisons between university and families on our annual University to Career Day. On this day, fifth grade students and parents spend a day on our university campus touring, visiting classes, speaking to admission counselors in their native language, and gathering information about the university's application process. Families come away with knowledge of the university system and tools to navigate the process. Students begin to see university as a possibility, and learn the mantra ¡Sí, se puede! [Yes, you can!] (Gómez et al., 2012).

CHALLENGES AND OPPORTUNITIES

As with any initiative involving multiple entities, competing agendas often arise. The most common challenges existing between an institution of higher education and a PDS are scheduling, communication, and commitment. Without a shared vision and clear expectations of the school's and university's responsibilities, resentment and frustration can percolate. Over time, if unaddressed, these challenges slowly erode many of the fundamental elements necessary to partnerships in community schools.

For the most part, opportunities outweigh the challenges. Gradually, excitement builds when the school community realizes the untapped potential of preparing teachers in their setting. Once the PDS is embedded within the school community, stakeholders quickly discover the multitude of opportunities pre-service teachers provide in all facets of the school day. Principals, teachers, and partners come to rely upon the presence of pre-service teachers to elevate the school's learning community profile. Initial trepidation becomes a willingness to explore the reciprocal benefits pre-service teacher preparation provides teachers, professors, partners, students, and families.

Funding

Funding for pre-service teacher preparation requires a commitment from the school and university to share in-kind services. In many instances, rather than a financial obligation, both parties agree to reallocate resources and offer in-kind services. More often than not, the reciprocal nature of partnership provides a win-win for both parties. After identifying respective needs, policies and practices are jointly created to build an infrastructure for sustainability, often with the support and guidance of the PDS leadership team.

Ideally, the school provides access to space/classrooms, collaborating teachers, students, parents, partners, and district support. The university reconsiders its role as merely a campus-based institution focused on theory and its application to the classroom to one of providing site-based courses and practice in community schools. In doing so, faculty members are assigned to a community school where education courses are taught, teacher candidates are supervised in classrooms, research is conducted, and professional development opportunities for all stakeholders are nurtured. This brings extra resources from the university partner into community schools that need the help.

Sustainability of the Role

Relationships are the linchpin of a PDS/community school partnership. Given the multiple individuals who impact pre-service teachers it is important to regularly nurture these relationships. When done right, each person sees themselves as responsible for raising the next generation of teachers. As might be expected when individuals share a common goal, key champions emerge to move the work forward. It is the individual champions from each partnership working collaboratively through acts of "paying it forward" who ultimately strengthen and sustain the partnership.

FINAL THOUGHTS

In her seminal work on cultural conflict in the classroom, Delpit (2006) posited that teachers cannot begin to understand their students unless they connect with families and communities; further noting that teachers will not value the knowledge that parents and community members bring unless such knowledge has been modeled for them by those who prepare them to teach.

Linda Darling-Hammond and her colleagues write, "Studies of experiential community-based learning opportunities for prospective teachers have noted that they can develop positive dispositions and attitudes toward children and families that carry over to teaching" (Darling-Hammond, Hammerness, Grossman, Rust, & Shulman, 2005, p. 417). It is within this broader context of learning how to teach in a community school that favorable attitudes and dispositions toward families and community members are nurtured.

Collaboration between community schools that participate with a university prepares pre-service teachers for the complexities of teaching, in general, and the teaching of the whole child, specifically. Each thoughtfully crafted partnership interaction has the potential to transform pre-service teachers' beliefs about underlying factors of children's overall success and thereby influence their practice.

The model presented provides ample opportunities for pre-service teachers to work at the "elbow' of others": professors, classroom teachers, peers, and partner agencies, to support whole child education and the community school strategy. The community school/PDS model can be the vital link which connects the community and its partners to the preparation of future teachers—the kind of teachers our most underserved schools require. It is our firm belief that community schools are the next frontier to develop cultural competency and build an equity-oriented mind-set during the teachers' pre-service years.

REFERENCES

Anderson, L., & Stillman, J. (2011). Student teaching for a specialized view of professional practice? Opportunities to learn in and for urban, high-needs schools. *Journal of Teacher Education, 62* (5), 446–465.

Bankston, C. L., & Caldas, S. J. (2017). Race, equity, and social capital in the changing suburbs. In S. B. Wepner & D. W. Gómez (Eds.), *Challenges facing suburban schools: Promising responses to changing student populations* (pp. 15–30). Lanham, MD: Rowman & Littlefield.

Council of Chief State School Officers. (2011). InTASC model core teaching standards: A resource for state dialogue. Retrieved from InTASC_Model_Core _Teaching_Standards_2011.pdf.

Darling-Hammond, L. (1994). Professional development schools: Early lessons, challenges, and promises. In L. Darling-Hammond (Ed.), *Professional development schools: Schools for developing a professional* (pp. 1–27). New York: Teachers University Press.

Darling-Hammond, L. (2006). Powerful teacher education: Lessons from exemplary programs. San Francisco; CA. Jossey-Bass.

Darling-Hammond, L., Hammerness, K., Grossman, P., Rust, F., & Shulman, L. (2005, p. 417). The design of teacher education programs. In L. Darling-Hammond and J. Bransford (Eds.), *Preparing teachers for a changing world* (pp. 390–441). San Francisco, CA: Jossey.

Delpit, L. (2006). *Other people's children: Cultural conflict in the classroom.* New York: The New Press.

Ferrara, J. (2014). *Professional development schools: Creative solutions for educators.* Lanham, MD: Rowman & Littlefield Education.

Ferrara, J., & Gómez, D. W. (2014). Broadening the scope of PDS liaisons' roles in community schools. *School-University Partnerships, 7*(1), 101–117.

Ferrara, J., Santiago, E., & Siry, C. (2008). Preparing teachers to serve diverse learners: A PDS/full-service community school model. In I. Guadarrama, J. Ramsey, & J. Nath (Eds.), *Professional Development Schools research, Volume 3*. Greenwich, CT: Information Age Publishing, 151–161.

Gómez, D. W., Ferrara, J., Santiago, E., Fanelli, F., & Taylor, R. (2012). Full-service community schools: A district's commitment to educating the whole child. In A. Honigsfeld & A. Cohan (Eds.), *Breaking the mold of education for culturally and linguistically diverse students: Innovative and successful practices for the 21st century* (pp. 65–73). Lanham, MD: Rowman & Littlefield Education.

Howard, T. C. (2010). *Why race and culture matter: Closing the achievement gap in America's classrooms.* New York: Teachers University Press.

Moir, E., Berlin, D., Gless, J, & Miles, J. (2009). New teacher mentoring: Hopes and promise for improving teacher effectiveness. Cambridge, MA: Harvard Education Press.

Santiago, E., Ferrara, J., & Blank, M. (2008). A full-service school fulfills its promise. *Educational Leadership, 65*(7), 44–47.

Wepner, S. B., Gómez, D. W., & Ferrara, J. (2013). Beyond campus walls for preparing new teachers to work with Hispanic students. *Excelsior: Leadership in Teaching and Learning, 8*(1), 95–105.

Zeichner, K. (2010). Rethinking the connections between campus courses and field experiences in college- and university-based teacher education. *Journal of Teacher Education, 61*(1-2), 89–99.

Chapter Five

The Community School Coordinator

Connecting Hearts and Mission

Lissette Gomez

The community school strategy requires a paradigm shift in culture, moving from a traditional public school model, where the principal is the sole leader and makes all final decisions, to a model where there is shared leadership between the principal, community-based partners, families, staff, young people, and community members. This shift requires the addition of a transformational leadership role that pays particular attention to the social and emotional factors that impact learning, the role of partnerships in enhancing learning, and authentic family and community engagement. This role is best recognized as a community school coordinator.

The role of a community school coordinator, oftentimes known for coordinating resources and partnerships, actually does much more. The role includes conducting strategic planning and action, navigating complex relationships, building trust, and responding proactively to a dynamic political, economic, and social environment. This form of leadership requires a transformational approach that builds authentic and collaborative partnerships, brings keen attention to human interactions and operational factors, and creates a holistic vision to guide change in communities.

Community school initiatives across the country refer to this leadership role in different ways, such as the community school director, community school coordinator, resource coordinator, resource navigator, or resource manager. Some coordinators work for lead agencies. Others are employed directly by school districts or citywide intermediary organizations. Despite the variation in title and who hires them, the responsibilities are the same. The coordinator works with others to understand how schools and their stakeholders advocate for change.

Their work focuses on inspiring, motivating, and aligning people around a more holistic strategy that incorporates a vision of success and results, based on the views and voices of all stakeholders: the students, staff, parents, and community. The community school coordinator strategically identifies necessary resources and partnerships and creates key infrastructure and supports that lead to greater outcomes for all students. For this chapter, I will use the term community school director (CSD) most often.

I invite you on a journey that is guided by passion, insights, and lessons learned from my experience as a CSD over a period of five years at P.S. 5, The Ellen Lurie School—a Children's Aid community school in New York City.[1] The core philosophy, fundamental practices, and the complexities involved in successfully leading and sustaining solid school-community partnerships will come to life through my reflections on my experience. In addition, my colleague and current community school coordinator, Liz Thacker, from Knoxville, Tennessee, will also share her journey. I trust that this chapter will not only bring you a fresh perspective, but also ignite a renewed sense of purpose about, and commitment to, what it truly takes to successfully lead a community school.

A DAY IN THE LIFE OF A COMMUNITY SCHOOL DIRECTOR

A community school coordinator's day varies depending on the school, staff, partners, activities, and whatever else a day in a busy school may bring. The following is a snapshot of a typical day in my life as a director of a Children's Aid full-service community school:

The bell rings and its 7:30 a.m., I am off to the school leadership team meeting. As the community school director, I am a crucial member of the school's governance structures, whether formal or informal. Formal meetings are essential and informal meetings happen organically and are just as important. I also sit on several committees such as the school leadership team; principal's cabinet; pupil personnel team; and school safety committee; and other governance and planning bodies whose work is relevant to building a responsive and cohesive school-community partnership.

My role is to facilitate and plan key committee meetings, especially those that bring in family and community partners. My school recognizes my role as essential for aligning partnerships around its vision and results.

After the first meeting of the day, I step into the family room to greet our families. I informally gather information about what is happening in the community and make connections. Some of the interactions and activities I often encounter in the family room are: grandparents engaged in conversations about the struggles they face raising their grandchildren, a teacher meeting with the social worker and advocating for services for families in crisis, the principal greeting new families and orientating them to the school philosophy, policies, and pedagogy, or the parent coordinator preparing for a workshop for families with children in the early childhood program.

The family room is the heartbeat of my community school. It's where families connect with one another and with the school staff and where services are accessed and families feel safe and valued. This dedicated space for families is a key part of the strategy for creating a welcoming environment in the school that belongs to families. Based on my knowledge of the family engagement research and Dr. Karen Mapp's Dual Capacity Framework, it is important to have families feel that the program is theirs and that it belongs to them. Their space should be their comfort zone, not the back of the cafeteria or a hallway; a place that's welcoming and a resource space for them.

Around 11:00 a.m., I am prepping for the weekly meeting with my principal—on the agenda is the academic needs of our English Language Learners (ELL), alignment of the after-school program with the school day and parent-teacher conferences. Securing regular meetings with the principal sends a strong message to school staff, families, partners, and other key stakeholders about prioritizing the community school strategy. During these meetings, I am able to demonstrate my value to the school's success and how I complement the principal's essential role.

Around 1:00 p.m., I head out to meet with the leadership at a local shelter to discuss how to improve communication and collaboration in order to better serve the needs of the children and their families in temporary housing. I am able to bring back this information to our attendance meeting with school staff and develop a tiered plan for how to best support these students.

During the after-school program, I observe the program activities to ensure that instruction and learning are of the highest quality and are aligned with the school day. I meet with the program's director to debrief the observation, highlight best practices and develop a plan for how to align the program with the school day and address the areas in need of improvement. As a bridge between the "school day" and "after-school," I am uniquely positioned to make connections that enhance student learning. Research tells us that the hours outside the traditional "school day" are key to child and youth development. Many young people remain unsupervised and engage in anti-social, high-risk behaviors during the hours of 3–6 p.m. (Little, Wimer, & Weiss, 2008). These hours add up to a substantial amount of time for learning in ways that can be new and refreshing or as a reinforcement of key skills learned but not practiced during the school day. All of these reasons demonstrate an outstanding opportunity to provide youth with additional time on task, time in caring relationships with others, and time with a caring adult—all resulting in positive outcomes. Community schools create the conditions for expanded learning opportunities that provide a continuum of community engagement opportunities and address real-world learning and community problem-solving through strategic partnerships. The CSD builds relationships and mechanisms to effectively link the school day to expanded learning activities.

My final meeting of the day is with the Parent Teacher Association, where we are planning our back to school night and strategizing how to increase family engagement in our school. I create additional opportunities for families to amplify their voices and help lead the community school work.

As I prepare to leave for the day at 6:15 p.m., the program director informs me that one of the students in after-school has not been picked up. I return to the office and begin to call the student's emergency phone number. As a Community School Director, I have to be an adaptive leader in order to provide the right resources, to the right students, at the right time.

As you can see, a so-called typical day can easily become not so common. As a transformational and adaptive leader, the CSD must be able to tolerate uncertainty; be adaptive and responsive in making environmental shifts; ask tough questions; remain persistent in the face of setbacks; and be able to observe what is going on from different perspectives before taking action. This latter skill is often described in the adaptive leadership literature as the ability to "get on the balcony" where you can see the larger picture in all its complexity (Heifetz & Linksy, 2014). This leadership style must communicate confidence, mobilize communities to tackle hard challenges, and execute change while celebrating strengths and successes.

LEADERSHIP SKILLS

The role of the CSD is versatile by design, embedding itself into many facets of the operation of the school. A CSD requires a wide range of complex skills—skills that draw on and combine strong leadership and management abilities. My organization defines the role in *Leading with Purpose and Passion: A Guide for Community School Directors* from the National Center for Community Schools (NCCS) thusly:

> The Community School Director is a leader who empowers, builds, creates and develops relationships with school leaders, stakeholders, and community organizations in order to implement a community school strategy guided by a community school plan. The Community School Director bridges the relationships between all stakeholders to improve connectedness and surround the whole child with support—academically, socially, emotionally, and physically. (Children's Aid National Center for Community Schools, 2018)

While the exact job descriptions of community school coordinators around the country may vary, they typically share the responsibilities characterized above.

Drawing upon NCCS work with community school initiatives around the country, Children's Aid identified and has organized the skills of a CSD around the core strategic functions of a community school. These skills are critical to developing responsive and results-oriented supports and services for students and their families. The CSD must have the ability to:

Leadership and Capacity

- Cocreate, hold, and articulate the community school's shared vision
- Facilitate the development of trusting relationships across the school (including with community partners)
- Share leadership with the school's principal and leadership team
- Identify and build support for new opportunities
- Identify and negotiate solutions to challenges
- Respond and adapt to changing conditions

Data-Driven Decision Making

- Identify and access key data sources
- Lead the school's annual needs and assets assessment
- Use data to respond to identified strengths and needs
- Use data to focus on results and continuous improvement

Advocacy and Policy Change

- Identify and engage key champions, including elected officials (but if they don't have the skill level, this is where their supervisor or agency may need to back them)
- Communicate and demonstrate the value of the community school strategy

Communications

- Represent the community school in multiple forums
- Listen and respond actively to key constituencies

Resource Development and Coordination

- Be the "411"—know who is who and where everything is. The CSD should be a key source of information.
- Identify needs and opportunities.
- Leverage, organize, and align school and community resources. The CSD is the key alignment in the triangle of home, school, and community. The CSD is the connector, the thread, and the connective tissue between all the other key stakeholders.
- Manage and align partners around agreed-upon results. This takes compromise and fighting against co-competition which is bound to exist but doesn't have to be the way we operate. We want win-win partnerships where all are valued and all get something they want, true nature of collaboration.
- Develop, and control expenses within, a site-based budget. There should be a shared budget focused on the goals of what you want for children regardless of whose budget it comes from. For example, in Newark, New Jersey, the Quitman Community School shared an accountant who

took the school's and lead agency's budgets and said, just tell me what you want to happen for kids, that's how we will decide how to use the budgets, and the rest they had to fund-raise for.

Community Engagement and Coordination

- Identify and build strong working relationships with needed community resources.
- Identify untapped community resources.
- Identify assets in families and communities.
- Create leaders and empower parents and families to self-advocate and create change.
- Build youth leadership and voice. Use "grow our own" strategies to develop future leaders of school and community.
- Organize community resources around student success.

Some of these points, such as leadership and capacity, communication, community engagement, and coordination will be described in greater details in the sections that follow. As an advisor to the principal, the CSD is responsible for the implementation and integration of the community school and provides strategic leadership that aligns partners and coordinates the work at the site-level. The CSD also works with the principal, School Leadership Team, and the parent coordinator to implement a transformative model of family engagement that creates strong school-to-home partnerships for learning and healthy development.

THE PRINCIPAL AND DIRECTOR PARTNERSHIP

One of the most important relationships a CSD needs to develop and to nurture is with the principal. The principal is the primary school leader and gatekeeper for initiatives, partnerships, and resources. As described in chapter 2, a community school principal is one who shares ownership and decision making. The working relationship between the principal and the CSD can make or break a community school.

Based on our work at Children's Aid with many initiatives across the country, we have observed that in newer initiatives, it takes time for the principal to share his or her "authority" with the CSD, making it harder for the director to thrive in the true "partner" role. Only the principal can really give this authority or create the culture where the school staff sees the CSD as an equal partner. It is imperative that a principal publicly notes and recognizes the CSD as their "partner" by having the CSD act as a representative of the partnership in internal and external meetings, communication materials such as shared letterheads, and letters that go out jointly and in other forms of communication to the public and stakeholders.

By managing strategic partnerships and identifying community resources, the director helps the principal by bringing in resources that address what's needed to achieve the comprehensive improvement plan and goals of the school. When the director and principal meet, they review the school improvement plan and goals.

They use their strategic planning time to concentrate on the development and implementation of a high-quality core instructional program that is aimed at improving the whole child, improving learning through all developmental domains, and ensuring that the instructional practices and programs provide what is needed across all the developmental domains.

Fifteen years after leaving the role of a CSD, I asked myself, "What made the partnership with my principal successful?" For starters, my office was inside the main office, right next to the principal's office, a strategic decision that facilitated constant communication formally and informally. It didn't matter that the space was small, had served as a copier room, and had no windows. This prime location served several purposes: it provided proximity to the principal and her management staff; it gave my role as director implicit authority; it demonstrated publicly the importance of the director relationship to the principal; and this prime real estate added credibility to the community school strategy.

After all these years, the CSD's office at P.S. 5 is still at the same location. And even when the school has offered a bigger, sunny space for the CSD elsewhere, Children's Aid, the lead agency, kept this ideal location because it is strategically perfect. One important role of the CSD is to negotiate the best space available having both the programmatic and strategic needs in mind.

Developing relationships with the principal takes time for all CSDs. Over time, my partnership with the principal evolved to one of mutual respect, appreciation, support, and most of all, authenticity. Yet this stature was not something that was immediately given with the title of director and the location of my office. I remember our first encounter when she told me, "The buck stops here, it's my way or the highway," as she demanded more test preparation in after-school.

It was a humbling moment. I didn't see her as an adversary. I understood then that she was invested in her students' success and wanted to ensure that they had the necessary supports and resources. I found myself asking the principal for guidance as I became familiar with the academic standards and was able to link learning after-school to the school day's academic goals.

Once I was able to demonstrate that we were working toward the same results, the principal was able to see the added value of our enrichment approach and how the programs strengthened student learning. The relationship shifted to one of mutual respect and trust. There was synergy between us that made it easier to make decisions, raise concerns, and explore new opportunities. The relationship with the principal is where my work started, but working with partners is what makes a community school unique.

BROKERING AND SUSTAINING INTENTIONAL PARTNERSHIPS

Remember, community schools create a shared vision and bring together the community's best thinking and resources to address the barriers that impede learning and healthy development. The CSD is responsible for facilitating an assets/needs assessment process that engages multiple stakeholders in gathering a wide range of data to inform and drive decisions about the community school's programming and operations. Before developing a community school's work plan, the coordinator must recognize what is working and not working.

This is integral to the process and ensures the right partners are working with the right people at the right time. The assessment process should be ongoing and must be revisited regularly by all partners in order to build on the strengths of the community and meet documented needs.

While the CSD can help lead this process, they cannot do it alone. The CSD partners with the school's principal, school leadership team,[2] staff, families, young people, and other key stakeholders to analyze school data and to combine data sources to give stakeholders a more complete picture of what the community school is accomplishing and needs.

Throughout this process, the school leadership team analyzes the school's data by combining and assessing data sources that can give all the stakeholders a fuller picture of what the community school is accomplishing and needs to do in the future. In community school initiatives, such as in New York City, CSDs have access to school and student data on a confidential basis, which allows the leadership team to understand and respond to both student-level and whole school needs, as well as to assess the results of specific interventions.

This access is critical in ensuring a focus on continuous improvement and results-based accountability. Without coordination and alignment, community schools run the risk of creating a haphazard collection of programs and partners that are working in silos rather than growing deep intentional ties between school, family, and community.

Community schools are planned, implemented, and maintained by active and coordinated partners that are dedicated to improving all domains of health and well-being. To successfully broker and sustain partnerships, the director applies a diagnostic, managerial, and integrated problem-solving approach. After facilitating a comprehensive needs and assets assessment, the CSD and principal select the right partners to respond to the identified needs and the school's strategic plan.

Once the appropriate partners are identified, the CSD manages all aspects of the partnership to make sure partners' use of time and space is well coordinated. Finally, the CSD ensures partners' services and resources are seamlessly integrated with the school's core instructional plan and mission.

Successful partnerships between the schools and community organizations are key ingredients to supporting young people and their families. Each partnership establishes an aligned mission and vision, mutually agreed-upon goals, shared decision making, and shared accountability. The benefit of working in a partnership is that there is synergy that motivates, inspires, and propels movement toward change. These partnerships not only support learning, they also provide students and their families access to continuity of services and a range of expanded learning opportunities and developmental supports with multiple entry points into the school day to support student learning.

Through these partnerships, the school culture and climate is strengthened and the academic curriculum is complemented with a wider range of services and activities designed to address barriers to learning. Ultimately, there is better alignment of programming and services to support a shared vision for learning and development, and resources are maximized and targeted. What's unique to partnerships in a community school compared to a traditional school is that the CSD is able to identify and support expert, intentional, aligned, and results-focused partnerships.

While you cannot plan for every roadblock along the way, there are some basic steps to make partnerships run smoothly: plan together from the start, clarify the vision, take time to get to know one another, set group norms, start small, build gradually, involve families as partners, clarify roles and responsibilities, share decision making, prepare team members to work together, stay flexible, keep tending the relationship, and be strategic.

FAMILY PARTNERSHIP

Family engagement is a crucial factor in the success of a community school. It is an ongoing effort that requires a shift in thinking that moves away from seeing families as part of the problem, to partners in crafting solutions. Successful family engagement efforts depend on a high level of trust between families and community school staff and partners. When families and caretakers have trust in you, they are more likely to participate and be engaged.

As partners in student learning and development, families must be engaged in ways that are meaningful and authentic. We must recognize family members' needs and challenges, but also value the assets and resources they bring to both children's development and learning. Families should be invited to the table as partners, decision makers, and advisors whenever possible. They should also join in celebrations of student achievement or progress, just as schools invite families in to address student needs or concerns. Community school directors and their teams often serve as a bridge between families and other key school personnel. They also provide a crucial layer of support to family members.

A CSD often shares what seems like informal conversations in the family room with parents, grandparents, teachers, and other staff over endless cups of coffee. These "informal" conversations provide insights into the dreams, assets, and areas of opportunity within the community. This "informal" but conscious assessment can often result in concrete programmatic solutions.

For instance, at Children's Aid, the school leadership team realized that more grandparents were frequenting the family room. A grandparents' group was created to provide a network of support and access to services that helped them raise their grandchildren. This investment in authentic connections with families and the community fostered an environment where everyone felt respected, connected, and valued. CSDs help transform schools into community hubs where all families and community members can access programs like English as a Second Language, General Education Development (GED), financial literacy, wellness courses, as well as other community resources.

BUILDING CAPACITY AND STRENGTHENING LEADERSHIP FOR COMMUNITY SCHOOL DIRECTORS

The work of a CSD is complex, dynamic, challenging, and—at times— overwhelming. As a catalyst for change, the CSD plays an important role in creating alignment around the community school strategy, building systems of accountability, and inspiring the community around opportunities and success.

Given the complexities and demands of the work, Children's Aid understood early on that a full-time CSD was essential to the strategy's success. A key lesson learned during the initial years of our community schools implementation was the critical value of providing CSDs with the direction, guidance, and support they needed. As a result, we created a management infrastructure that included a division director who provides overall leadership to the community schools and a cadre of deputy directors who provide ongoing coaching and weekly supervision, each one working with a cohort of schools in a similar geographic region. This

TEXTBOX 5.1. KNOXVILLE'S TENNESSEE'S PERSPECTIVE

Liz Thacker

It doesn't take long in the role as a community school coordinator to realize that you are not in this alone. It really does take a village to successfully implement and manage a community school! One of the most important relationships is that of the principal and the coordinator, as ideally you truly share leadership. A principal is the person who oversees all the academic data whereas coordinator manages all the partners. When this relationship is seamless, and a principal sees the value and purpose of a coordinator, it becomes much easier to navigate through the school and the staff. Shared leadership allows for easier implementation of community school ideas and programs.

A great relationship makes the work that much easier. However, challenges arise when the principal does not view the coordinator in a position of shared leadership. Valuable time is wasted if an unsupportive administrator undermines the work. Regardless of whether the relationship is ideal or lacking, communication between a coordinator and an administrator is key! It is also important for the coordinator to establish and leverage his/her own relationships with other staff members who help champion the work.

Community schools in Knoxville first came about in the late 1990s under the direction of Dr. Robert Kronick full-service schools at three inner-city elementary schools. In 2010, Knoxville had its first University Assisted Community School (UACS) at Pond Gap Elementary school with help from Dr. Kronick and funding from local businessman Randy Boyd. In 2011, the community increased its interest and support to expand on all the great things happening at Pond Gap. The United Way of Greater Knoxville sponsored a trip to Cincinnati to take a closer look at their model of community schools. In the fall of 2012, Knoxville opened three more community schools under three different lead agencies—Norwood Elementary (Great Schools Partnership), Lonsdale Elementary (Project Grad), and Greene Magnet Academy (YMCA).

In the 2017–2018 school year, the Knoxville Initiative has fifteen community schools (thirteen under the direction of Great Schools Partnership [GSP] and two under the direction of the University of Tennessee as University Assisted Community Schools). Of the thirteen under GSP, two are middle schools and eleven are elementary schools. Great Schools Partnership currently employs thirteen coordinators, one for each community school. Our coordinators report to one of two field supervisors who not only support our coordinators, but help with the initiative as a whole. Both of our field supervisors report to GSP's Vice President of Operations.

One of the many great things about our initiative is that as we have expanded into the middle school realm, we took into account existing feeder

(continued)

TEXTBOX 5.1.   *(continued)*

patterns. Both of our middle schools are comprised of several feeder schools that are also community schools. This allows for great communication and collaboration of coordinators for the betterment of our students, families, and communities.

Our GSP Board includes both of our mayors (city and county), our super-intendent of schools, the dean of the University of Tennessee, the president of Pellissippi State Community College, the Chamber of Commerce, the Urban League, and various local businesses and church-based personnel. Just like our board, the community school initiative is extremely diverse in our partner-ships. At this time, we have over 100 partners that work with one or more of our sites.

These partnerships include aftercare providers, faith-based organization, mental health organizations, dental clinics, local business, and various other organizations throughout the community. Like our board and our partnerships, funding for our initiative comes from a variety of places. We receive both city and county funding (both of our mayors are huge community school advo-cates), as well as funding support from the United Way and private donors.

Each of our community schools have two site-based teams: the site steering committee and the partner coalition. The site steering committee is comprised of educators, parents, and community members who develop the vision for the school. Community partners take part in the partner coalition where they take the vision set by the steering committee and help carry out the mission. As a coordinator, I work with both teams.

In closing, let me leave you with some advice. Be present! A coordinator is only as good as the relationships he/she has formed. That occurs from being around and being present and accessible. Be approachable! A coordinator really is the connector between all the various entities—school, students, parents, partners, and community—and they all need to be able to approach you. Be patient! The work of a coordinator is not accomplished overnight, but rather by the day in and day out work that adds up. Communicate! Most of a coordinator's job revolves around communication. It is important to keep all entities in the know. And lastly—have fun! This work is very demanding, but it is also extremely rewarding!!

central team also provides assistance with budgeting, program quality, and on-site problem-solving.

Children's Aid chose the title of "director" and decided to further el-evate the role by hiring master's level professionals in the areas of social work or related fields (e.g., education, public administration) with at least five to seven years of experience. This decision has influenced how principals from initiatives across the country engage with directors as seasoned strategic partners that align programs and services with the school's educational mission and outcomes, and are sometimes even capable of leading the community school in their absence.

An effective onboarding process for a CSD is important to ensuring their success. As part of their orientation, the director should receive an overview on what is a community school and the best practices and principles that guide implementation of the strategy. Ongoing professional development aims to help CSDs to improve their performance and increase their capabilities of successfully leading a community school.

These professional development offerings can include monthly peer convening, topical workshops, and intensive training institutes. Each professional learning experience should meet the CSDs' individual needs, provide time to assimilate new knowledge, and practice new skills.

Through the coaching process, agency or district supervisors and outside technical assistance providers help CSDs learn strategies to manage the demands of the work, create and maintain balance, and develop enough confidence to enable them to let others lead alongside them. Strengthening and building the capacity of a CSD in many ways mirrors the work of a community school's development: its success depends on identifying strengths and needs, building relational trust, joint planning, ongoing assessment, and effective partnership.

FINAL THOUGHTS

As more cities embrace the community school strategy as a viable and responsive approach to education reform, an opportunity arises for harnessing the field's best practices, thinking, and evidence around what it takes to inspire and transform communities. Fortunately for current CSDs, there is now a strong body of experience and knowledge that have informed some of the latest professional development opportunities. For instance:

- Children's Aid National Center for Community Schools developed a guide for community school directors, *Leading with Purpose and Passion (Children's Aid National Center for Community Schools, 2018)*, a complementary training video, *A Day in the Life of a Community School*

Director (Children's Aid National Center for Community Schools, 2017), and a multi-day director leadership institute to help clarify and elevate the role and to provide practical advice and strategies about how to implement the role with intelligence, energy, purpose, and passion.

- The Coalition for Community Schools developed Community School Standards[3] to engage and support the community school movement as a standards-driven, evidence-based strategy to promote equity and educational excellence for each and every child, and an approach that strengthens families and community. In order to inform and guide the implementation continuum of a comprehensive and coherent community school strategy, CSDs should refer to the following standards:

  ○ Collaborative Leadership
  ○ Planning
  ○ Coordination Infrastructure
  ○ Student-Centered Data
  ○ Continuous Improvement
  ○ Authentic Family Engagement
  ○ Authentic Community Engagement

- The Coalition for Community Schools also facilitates the community school coordinators network which serves as a forum for community school coordinators to share ideas and experiences, ask questions and get answers, and have a centralized place to find resources and tools. The Coalition has built a website platform to provide the resources and a space for the network to interact and grow.
- The University of Chicago School of Social Service Administration offers the Leadership in Community Schools program, designed to educate social workers for new roles in urban schools, and more specifically, in the community school approach.
- In partnership with the Children's Aid National Center for Community Schools, Binghamton University offers the first-ever innovative online community schools advanced certificate program, designed for school professionals from across disciplines, community-based service providers, or anyone seeking a role that makes meaningful, measurable improvements in lives and communities.
- In September 2017, the Coalition for Community Schools partnered with the Netter Center for Community Partnerships, Communities in

Schools, the Beacon National Network, and the National Center for Community Schools to inaugurate Coordinator's Appreciation Week. It was a huge success. People from across the country poured out their thankfulness to their community school coordinators with funny gifts, ice cream socials, flowers, and heartfelt handwritten notes. This helps elevate and professionalize this important role in community schools.

When Children's Aid started this work in 1992, we had no models for this role, no job descriptions, no training or higher education courses, and no colleagues to shadow or consult. Today, community school coordinators are playing an increasingly important role in today's education reform. Binghamton University's graduate-level community school certification course, the University of Chicago School of Social Service Administration leadership program, NCCS's training materials, the New York City's Department of Education's Office of Community Schools, and standardization of the community school strategy at the systems level are all evidence that the role is professionalizing.

The community school field is in the maturing stage of development when it comes to the professionalization of coordinators. We must begin to move into the excelling stage of development to break down the silos, provide clarity about the role, and help coordinators move beyond coordination into a strategic leadership role.

The community school movement has experienced exponential growth as it has moved toward a comprehensive, results-orientated approach. After over a quarter century of implementation, we can see the long-term effect of what happens to children and families when you spark inspiration, provide opportunities, create a platform for voice and choice, and value the strengths and resources they bring to the community. This is when you understand the true power and impact that lie within community schools, and the powerful role the CSD plays in bringing the community school strategy to fruition.

As I reflect upon my experiences as a CSD (some 15 years ago), I recall the many immigrant families that made Washington Heights their home and their place of hope. In this neighborhood, the school quickly became a hub for children and families seeking the promise of possibilities that once seemed inaccessible to them because of the stress and isolation created by generational poverty, immigration status, and language isolation. The recipe for successfully turning a school into a robust learning hub must include a strong leader, the community school director.

REFERENCES

Children's Aid National Center for Community Schools. (2017). *A day in the life of a community school director*. Retrieved from https://www.youtube.com /watch?time_continue=5&v=7WNcrZrIU5E.

Children's Aid National Center for Community Schools. (2018). *Leading with purpose and passion: A guide for community school directors*. New York: Children's Aid National Center for Community Schools.

Heifetz, R. A., & Linksy, M. (2014). *Get on the balcony: Why leaders need to step back to get perspective*. Boston: Harvard Business Review Press.

Little, P. M. D., Wimer, C., & Weiss, H. B. (2008). *After school programs in the 21st century: Their potential and what it takes to achieve it. Issues and opportunities in out-of-school time evaluation. Number 10.* Harvard Family Research Project.

Chapter Six

Transformative Family Engagement in Community Schools

Megan Hester and Natasha Capers

What does it look like to utilize parents and communities to build community schools? It looks revolutionary. To create partnership, there must be an acknowledgment of a relationship of equal power. Parents may not bring the same things to the table, but they both bring something that is critical and needed. . . . Parents and community leaders will often be connected to a school longer than their principal, and it is important that they are brought into the decision-making processes and are engaged from beginning to end. Parents also bring critical information and resources to the table that are often overlooked because administrators have a lack of knowledge about the neighborhood.

—Natasha Capers, NYC Coalition for Educational
Justice Coordinator (Capers & Shah, 2015)

In parts of Africa, the palaver tree has played an important role in community building and local governance. The palaver is a large tree under whose shade the community gathers to discuss issues of common interest, solve community problems, and make decisions. Under the palaver, everyone has an equal right to speak, village life is collectively managed, and a cohesive community is built. Community schools can be the palaver tree for our communities.

Community schools can take many different forms. Some are deeply rooted in their neighborhood, reflecting and engaging the community in every aspect from school and program staffing, to curriculum and instruction, to after-school and weekend program design and more. Others are more traditional schools that house a collection of programs and services for students and families.

As staff who support the NYC Coalition for Educational Justice (CEJ), a grassroots coalition of parents organizing for excellent public schools in low-income Black and Latino communities, we believe that community schools should be places that not only meet the academic and non-academic needs of children, families, and the community, but also bring together multiple constituencies in the school and neighborhood—leadership, staff, parents, and community partners—to build community and make decisions as partners of equal power.

TRANSFORMATIVE ENGAGEMENT

Parents don't bring the *same* set of skills as teachers, administrators, or community organizations, but they bring one of the most important areas of expertise: their children, and the community and culture that shape their children every day. In a country where more than half of all public school students are students of color, but 82 percent of teachers and 80 percent of principals are white, schools that are not proactively tapping this expertise are crippling their efforts for educational excellence (U.S. Department of Education, 2016).

Deep partnership with families and communities—not as constituencies in need of assistance and services but as assets without whom the school's objectives cannot be met—is the soul of community schools, and what distinguishes community schools from schools that just house multiple programs and services. We call this type of partnership "transformative parent engagement" because it has the potential to fundamentally transform staff's relationships with children and their families; transform families' relationship to the school; transform students' experience in school; and transform school culture.[1]

Transformative parent engagement is characterized by practices that treat parents as:

- Experts on their children and their community. Parents bring a wealth of personal, cultural, and contextual knowledge and insight that teachers often don't have access to: sources of motivation for students, topics that students connect to, family routines that impact learning, culturally appropriate forms of communication, and much more.

- Partners in meaningful decision making on a wide range of issues. Parents can contribute in a variety of roles, from volunteers to key decision makers on school policy. The addition of multiple perspectives strengthens decisions and builds ownership around school policies and practices.
- Problem-solvers (rather than problems to be solved), and critical allies in reaching the school's academic goals. Parents bring insight, skills, and power that can be critical tools in tackling barriers to school success. This is true not only for the traditional parent engagement areas such as fund-raising and enrichment, but also core instructional issues. The same fearless, outspoken parent who is viewed as a problem by one school, can be viewed as a crucial source of information and a critical advocate by another school.
- Assets to their children and their community, with untapped knowledge and strengths. Parents—those with formal education and those without, those who speak English and those who don't, those with class privilege and those without—are a true gold-mine of resources and talent for schools. Some bring knowledge of education in their home countries that can innovate school practices; some bring skills of resilience and persistence that can strengthen and support students; some bring large networks of relationships that can be mobilized; and some bring fierce determination to secure what their children need. Many schools, however, do not know how to see and access that wealth.

This approach to parent engagement is supported by research (Stefanski, Valli, & Jacobson, 2016), and is reflected in the Coalition for Community Schools' Community School Standards.[2] In this chapter, we will detail some of the practices of transformative family engagement, and how community schools can integrate these practices into their structures and model.

TRADITIONAL ROLE OF FAMILIES IN TRADITIONAL SCHOOLS

In many urban schools, parents have traditionally been viewed as a nuisance who are better kept out of schools. In Anne Henderson's and Karen Mapp's framework of the four ways that schools approach parent engagement, they describe this approach as the "fortress school," which operates with a mentality of:

> Parents belong at home, not at school. If students don't do well, it's because their families don't give them enough support. We're already doing all we can. Our school is an oasis in a troubled community. We want to keep it that way. (Henderson & Mapp, 2002)

This type of approach is characterized by a deficit mentality toward families and communities—the idea that low-income students of color come from impaired homes and damaged communities that have few strengths and little value to share. This deficit mentality[3] is rooted in racial and class biases that many educators and schools hold—regardless of their own backgrounds—and are often unaware of.[4]

Teachers and school staff may feel that they are the experts on their students, and that they don't have anything to learn or gain from parents. The fact that the majority of public school teachers come from different racial and ethnic backgrounds than their students, and have been raised in a society saturated with biases and deficit thinking regarding low-income students of color, exacerbates this challenge. Research shows that biases impact the way that school staff perceive and respond to students on a daily basis, and affect disciplinary actions, assignment to advanced academic tracks, communication with parents, and many other aspects of school life.[5]

Mapp and Henderson name schools that have a slightly more open approach to parents as "come if we call" schools:

> Parents are welcome when we ask them, but there's only so much they can offer. The most important thing they can do is to help their kids at home. We know where to get community help if we need it. (Henderson & Mapp, 2002)

This type of school may not actively push parents out, but holds low expectations and doesn't see parents as assets who are critical to success. This approach reflects a charity-based mind-set, in which families and the community are primarily recipients of help, and the school/organizations are providers of that help. This approach is still rooted in deficit thinking, and is often perceived by parents as condescending and alienating.

Schools that are often seen as champions of parent engagement are characterized as "open door" schools:

Parents can be involved at our school in many ways—we're working hard to get an even bigger turnout for our activities. When we ask the community to help, people often respond. (Henderson & Mapp, 2002)

In this type of school, there are lots of activities happening for parents, and strong attendance by them. In many school systems, this level of engagement is held up as the model. However, engagement in these schools still happens on the school's terms: on topics that the school (rather than parents) determine to be important, at events that the school (rather than parents) plan and lead. Parents have minimal participation in real priority-setting and decision making for the school.

The type of school that community schools should aspire to is the "partnership school," which takes the approach:

All families and communities have something great to offer—we do whatever it takes to work closely together to make sure every single student succeeds. (Henderson & Mapp, 2002)

By taking this approach, community schools practice transformative parent engagement and embody the community school as the palaver tree. Schools work hard to develop trust with families; families are involved in major decisions; conflicts are resolved with all stakeholders together; school curricula, climate, and routines honor families' culture and contributions; school leadership and staff understand that they cannot achieve their goals without families as equal partners.

There is an expectation that parent engagement happens on parent turf, not just on school turf: school staff regularly go into the community or the home to meet parents where they are most comfortable, rather than expecting that parents always come to where staff are most comfortable. The school has moved from "we've got this without you" to "let's do this together" to "we can't do this without you."[6]

RESEARCH ON FAMILY ENGAGEMENT

Frameworks like this one from Henderson and Mapp are useful because while transformative parent engagement is rare, parent and community engagement is generally accepted as a core component of community schools, and has become a popular talking point in school reform generally. Elected officials, school districts, and school leaders like to say that they are committed to "parents as partners." What they mean by parent engagement, however, can differ wildly.

Just as simply having a teacher standing in front of students all day doesn't constitute effective teaching, having parent bodies inside a school building doesn't necessarily signify effective parent engagement. While extensive research has shown that effective methods of parent engagement can result in improved student attendance, achievement, and school climate, the method of parent engagement must have certain specific characteristics in order to produce those results. Dr. Mapp's research shows that in order to make an impact on school quality, parent engagement must be:

- Linked to learning: Linked with school and district achievement goals, and connecting families to teaching and learning (Westrich & Strobel, 2013).
- Relational: Focused on building trusting and respectful relationships between families and school staff. This involves addressing implicit and overt biases that shape staff interaction with families (Anderson, 2016).
- Developmental: Focused on building skills and experience of both school staff *and* parents to engage effectively with each other.
- Collective: Learning is in group settings and focused on building community.
- Interactive: Participants have opportunities to practice new skills and get feedback.

Dr. Mapp synthesized these elements in the Dual-Capacity Framework for Family-School Partnerships she developed for the U.S. Department of Education, which emphasizes that family engagement is a two-way street that requires schools to transform their approach and practices.[7] This is a paradigm shift from the traditional approach to parent engagement, which expects only families to change their approach and practices, without a corresponding change on the school's side.

TRANSFORMATIVE FAMILY ENGAGEMENT IN COMMUNITY SCHOOLS

Community schools have the opportunity to put the principles mentioned above into practice. We discuss some of the key strategies below.

Community schools use a collaborative school governance structure, in which parents are active and equal members of decision making. Many community schools have a community school team or other collaborative governance structure that involves parents, school staff, community-based organizations, and community members. However, without deep, ongoing work to build true collaboration as equals, parent participation on these bodies is often token; schools check a box to say that parents participated, without actually changing the culture and balance of power to allow those voices equal standing.

Because most members of the school governance structure are likely to be professionals with education degrees who are immersed in school issues and accustomed to sharing their ideas, it is necessary to provide support for parents on this structure if their participation is to be more than symbolic. This means planning the agenda ahead of time, talking with parents well before the meeting to explore the topics, providing background materials on issues being discussed, making space for the quieter voices, and facilitating discussions that are free of the jargon and acronyms that people outside of the education profession wouldn't understand.

The principal of a community school in the Washington Heights neighborhood of New York City acknowledged that while sharing power with parents is hard and he is often tempted to make school decisions quickly and unilaterally, he has committed to always bring parents into decisions even when it feels like a hassle, because he has found that the result is always better decisions, more successful implementation, and a stronger school community.

His approach reflects a respect for the knowledge that families bring to the table, as distinct and complementary to his own, and the understanding that it is only by combining the perspectives of educators *and* families that he can reach the best decisions for the school.

Community schools provide opportunities for parent leadership development, in order to equip parents for school and community leadership roles, and create a sustainable pipeline of leaders. Most community schools encourage parent *participation*—through attending and volunteering at school events or joining the parent association—but transformative parent engagement requires community schools to develop true parent *leadership*.

This means engaging and training parents on issues of education policy and practice that are critical for the school's progress and developing their knowledge about the power structure of the school district as well as skills such as how to advocate with the school district and elected officials, how to organize an agenda and facilitate a meeting, and how to speak in public.

For example, if a school is struggling with student achievement among eighth grade students, it is essential to seek the expertise of eighth grade parents about what their children need to excel, familiarize parents with methodologies for engaging adolescents academically, inform them about potential approaches to enhance the school's capacity in that area, solicit parents' ideas and insights, make a collective decision about how to address the problem, and build the skills needed to acquire the resources or policies to achieve improvement. As a result, the school improves its capacity and outcomes; and parents gain skills and knowledge that they can use in many other settings. Strong parent leaders can keep a school honest and accountable to the community school vision and model, regardless of the inevitable changes in education policy and school leadership.

Community schools utilize effective methods of parent outreach. Community schools must use personal, face-to-face and active methods to communicate with parents—for example:

- home visits, or meetups at a convenient location in the parents' neighborhood
- parent-to-parent phone calls
- teacher-to-parent phone calls
- face-to-face conversations with parents outside the school, in neighborhood stores, playgrounds, laundromats, religious institutions, bus and subway stops, barber shops, salons, etc.

While these methods are time-consuming, they are effective at building the relationships and connections that are essential for meaningful, sustained parent engagement, and worth the investment. The passive and impersonal outreach methods of fliers, robocalls, and emails may disseminate information but will never, ever build real and sustained parent engagement.

While fliers are useful to reinforce and remind people of information that has already been communicated face-to-face, very few people actually come to events based on a flier. And because easy access to email is dependent on resources, using email to communicate with parents can exclude less privileged families. Ultimately, meaningful parent engagement is based on relationships and personal connections, which fliers, emails, and robocalls do not achieve.

A community school in Brooklyn, New York, that serves a very diverse, multilingual community of families, was struggling with how to engage families who were not comfortable in English. They recruited one parent from each of the major language groups in the school to serve as the parent liaison for their community by conducting face-to-face outreach to their community, as well as providing translation and interpretation at parent meetings and one-on-one with teachers. The liaisons receive a small yearly stipend from Title 1 parent engagement funds, and are supported by school staff. As a result, engagement of immigrant parents has increased enormously at the school.

Community schools identify opportunities for school staff to learn about the school community. Research shows that teachers are much more effective in the classroom if they have a deep connection with the children they are teaching, and central to that is an understanding of the children's world—their families, their neighborhood, and their culture (Aronson and Laugnter, 2016).

Since, at most schools, the majority of teachers do not come from the same backgrounds as the students, school staff lack huge pieces of information and understanding about their students' lives and experiences. These deeper connections can be intentionally built if schools make a practice of staff leaving the building and going into the neighborhood. Some ways that schools can facilitate these types of experiences are:

• Organize community tours, in which parents and community members take school staff on a walking tour of the neighborhood to familiarize themselves with the community in which their students live and learn about local history, culture, and institutions.

- Compensate teachers to visit students' homes to get to know their students' families.[8]
- Encourage staff to visit local hangout spots like the playground, park, or basketball courts, and patronize local businesses, and meet people in the neighborhood.
- Organize field trips to local institutions to meet community leaders and learn about the neighborhood's past and present.
- Conduct regular, ongoing professional development on cultural responsiveness. This can take the form of reading and discussion groups, and more formal professional development with experts in the field.

Community school parents play a critical role in the community schools' needs/asset mapping, because they possess information about the strengths and struggles of the community that school staff do not have. The strategies mentioned above, as well as parent surveys, focus groups, and community forums are essential for the school to get a full picture of the community's needs and assets. Teachers benefit from all of these experiences, as they tap into community wisdom, increase their knowledge about their students' sociocultural context, and gain tools for connecting in-school learning to students' multiple identities and out-of-school lives.

On the school level, effective needs/asset mapping can generate information about local businesses that can donate to or partner with the school; local leaders that are critical to engage because of their knowledge and influence on families; past events—positive or negative—that impact families' relationship to the school; cultural practices and beliefs that impact students' and families' approach to the school; and most importantly, families' hopes and dreams for their child's education.

Community schools may also hold annual or biannual community forums in which school and CBO leadership and staff, together with parents and community members, come together to discuss how the school is doing and what the priorities should be for the next period. This opportunity to collect input from a broad swath of stakeholders builds school community, puts collaborative governance into action, and reinforces mutual accountability. In New York City, all community schools are required to hold community forums every spring in order to engage parents, students, school staff, and community members in reviewing progress over the past year, while setting priorities for the coming year.

A large-scale example of tapping community wisdom is the charrette process conducted by the A+NYC Coalition in New York City during the 2012–2013 school year. Led by parents and supported by staff from CEJ and the Alliance for Quality Education, parent leaders prepared for New York City's 2013 mayoral election by holding 75 community meetings in which parents, students, teachers, and community members discussed their vision for public schools. The comments from those community meetings were analyzed by a team of policy experts, who compiled them into a draft platform for education under the next mayor.

That draft platform was then mounted in a bright blue school bus that drove around the city to spots where parents could get on and vote for their highest priorities (Sangha, 2013). Ultimately, the highest voting items were included in an "Education Roadmap" report for the next mayor, which was presented to all the mayoral candidates for endorsement (A+ NYC, n.d.). Many of the candidates endorsed the document, and many of its recommendations were ultimately adopted by the new mayor.

Finally, all of these strategies mentioned above can have a significant positive impact on a community school's relationships with students, classroom management, and instructional quality (Bryk & Schneider, 2002; Bryk, Sebring, Allensworth, Easton, & Luppescu, 2010; Epstein & Sheldon, 2002; Henderson & Mapp, 2002; Westmoreland, Rosenberg, Lopez, & Weiss, 2009).

FAMILIES AS ASSETS

For a community school to become a partnership school, however, requires more than just a collection of activities; it requires a fundamental shift in mind-set to an asset-based way of thinking. This means taking the position that all families want the best for their child and will do everything they can to help that child be successful, and it means undoing harmful biases and stereotypes around a variety of characteristics such as race, appearance, family structure, socioeconomic status, language, country of origin, immigration status, and other identities.

For example, in some schools, it is seen as a deficit or a liability for a student to have parents who are monolingual Spanish-speakers (or any other language). The school might justify this by saying that the parents are difficult to get in contact with, don't read and respond to school notices and fliers, have limited formal education, or don't place a priority on their child's education, as evidenced by not attending school events.

This reasoning is steeped in assumptions and bias. In fact, it may likely be the school's failure to engage the family appropriately that is leading to the breakdown in communication: a lack of translation, a reliance on impersonal outreach such as fliers rather than personal contact, a lack of bilingual staff members to build a relationship with the family, and uninformed cultural assumptions.

Identifying and confronting these biases, and shifting to an asset mindset, would radically shift the school's relationship with Spanish-speaking families. A partnership school could look at this same family and see parents who are an asset because they foster bilingualism and biculturalism, model hard work and resilience in the face of challenges, and make sacrifices for their child's education.

This is just one example of the multiple ways that schools can view the very same parent. At one school, a parent can be seen as demanding and intrusive, while at another school the very same parent can be seen as proactive and committed. At one school, a parent can be thought of as uninvolved and uninterested, while at another school the very same parent can be seen as an untapped resource. The partnership school focuses on possibilities and progress, and magnifies strengths rather than challenges. This is not simple work, and requires proactively excavating and discarding the conscious and unconscious biases that we all carry around in some form.

THE ROLE OF THE COMMUNITY
SCHOOL COORDINATOR

While all community school leadership and staff must adopt this asset-based approach, the community school coordinator plays a critical role in modeling the approach, and helping move the school toward the partnership school approach (Fletcher, 2016). Some of the core skills necessary for the coordinator to do this, are:

- Understanding of the students' world (e.g., neighborhood, family and youth culture, economic/political/cultural/social dynamics that students and their families navigate);
- Ability to communicate effectively with multiple constituencies (e.g., school staff, CBO staff, parents, students, community allies) and to code-switch between them;
- Awareness of their own cultural/racial/social/gender identities and the impact of those identities personally and professionally, a desire to grow that awareness, and a commitment to engage others on these issues; and
- Belief that decisions made collectively are ultimately *better* decisions than those made individually; and a commitment to the labor-intensive work of collaborative governance.

Some community schools also have a family engagement coordinator in addition to the community school director, who carries out the legwork of outreach, relationship-building, leadership development, and programming for parents, so that the community school director can focus on programming and institutional partnerships for students. As mentioned above, some community schools also engage parents in that role, either as volunteers or with stipends paid through community school grants, Title 1, or other sources of funding.

There is no shortcut to authentic, transformative parent engagement. It requires the collaborative efforts of the community school director and partners to help build capacity. Often it can seem easier to revert to top-down decisions or to engage only those parents who fit within the school's comfort zone. Schools that are doing this work effectively know that it takes effort to live up to the vision of the community school as palaver tree; but the community they created together is well worth the investment.

PUTTING TRANSFORMATIVE PARENT ENGAGEMENT INTO ACTION

In this final section, we discuss concrete strategies that community schools can use to practice transformative parent engagement, including research-based models, parent advocacy, and staffing strategies.

Research-Based Models

Fortunately for community schools wanting to move toward a model of transformative parent engagement, there are proven models that are readily available. For instance:

- The Parent-Teacher Home Visit Project helps build relationships of mutual trust and respect between teachers and families through home visits in which parents and teachers build relationships as equal partners. In teams of two, teachers make 30-minute visits to families at their home, often during the summer before school starts. They ask questions to learn more about the family and the student and each person shares their hopes and dreams for the student. A follow-up visit is conducted in the spring to make plans for summer learning. Results nationally include increased parent involvement, more positive behavioral outcomes, and increased student achievement.[9]
- Academic Parent-Teacher Teams (APTT) makes the most of parent-teacher conferences through a structured design that trains families and teachers to link home and school learning. Teachers hold three 75-minute classroom meetings each year to share performance data for the class and individual student, model activities for families, and help parents practice these strategies and share other learning techniques they use at home. Parents are also invited for one 30-minute individual parent-teacher conference to review student performance data and create action plans to increase learning. National data show academic gains from schools using APTT as well as higher participation rate in parent-teacher conferences, especially among fathers.[10]
- The Parent Mentor Program, created by the Logan Square Neighborhood Association in Chicago, develops parents' skills and strategies to support their students academically, and assists teachers, by placing parents in classrooms to work with struggling students one-on-one. Parents receive weekly trainings on the school curriculum, teaching strategies for working with struggling students, and other information about the school system and then turnkey this information by offering four workshops a year to other parents. After completing 100 hours, parents receive a small stipend and opportunities for college credit, leading toward certification as a paraprofessional or teacher. Results

from implementation in Illinois show increased parent involvement, improved parent confidence and competence supporting learning, and student progress.[11]

- Abriendo Puertas is a parent training program developed by and for Latino parents with children ages zero to five. The program uses popular education methodology and culturally relevant curriculum to engage parents in lessons about early child development, local schools, literacy and math skills, social-emotional wellness, and parent leadership. After the initial 10 sessions, parents can be trained an additional three days to be trainers for other parents, and thus scale up the model.[12]

Parent Advocacy

Parents are advocates to protect the policies, practices, and funding streams necessary to create, sustain, and expand community schools. Community schools that build parent leadership also build a constituency that can push elected officials, school districts, foundations, and other power players to support community schools—especially when schools and community-based organizations are not in a position to advocate themselves.

Parent advocacy can take many forms. Community school parents can play a role in advocating for:

- District, city, or state funding and other resources for community schools
- City or state legislation supporting community schools
- Resources that are essential to community school success, such as health clinics, bilingual teachers, college counselors, etc.
- Policies that define and protect community schools across changes in political administrations
- Policies that clear barriers to the smooth operation of community schools, for example, regarding licensing, contracting, hiring, or other obstacles

It is important that this advocacy is shaped and led by parents themselves—not just by staff using parents' stories as ammunition. In this way, parents have the opportunity to step into greater leadership, build personal and institutional power, and develop skills that they can use in many different settings. Building parents' advocacy skills embodies principles of transformative parent engagement because it is a practice of moving from

TEXTBOX 6.1. PARENT RESOURCES

Community Schools Toolkit
http://populardemocracy.org/sites/default/files/Community-Schools-Toolkit.pdf

Four Types of Family-School Partnerships
http://www.ilcommunityschools.org/images/files/BeyondtheBakeS_rubric%20
-%20Sarah%20Ogeto%20ISBE.pdf

http://www.edweek.org/ew/section/infographics/the-pathway-to-a-partnership
-school.html

Building Family-School Alliances for Effective Parent Engagement
https://parentactionbx.wixsite.com/parentalliances

The Power of Community Schools
http://vue.annenberginstitute.org/issues/40/power-community-schools

Beyond Involvement and Engagement: The Role of the Family in School-Community Partnerships
https://files.eric.ed.gov/fulltext/EJ1124001.pdf

Role of Program Staff in Successful Family Engagement Activities
http://vue.annenberginstitute.org/issues/44/making-space-collaboration-and
-leadership-role-program-staff-successful-family-engagemen-0

Empowering Parents and Building Communities: The Role of School-Based Councils in Educational Governance and Accountability
http://journals.sagepub.com/doi/pdf/10.1177/0042085907305044

Family Engagement Resources from the Global Family Research Project
https://globalfrp.org/Our-Work/Family-Engagement

Capturing the Ripple Effect: Developing a Theory of Change for Evaluating Parent Leadership Initiatives
https://www.annenberginstitute.org/sites/default/files/capturingtherippleeffect
reportweb.pdf

the traditional, charity-based model of doing *for* families to the transformative, collaborative model of doing *with* families.

One example of parent advocacy in action is in 2014, after a multi-year campaign for community schools by parents and community organizations, Mayor Bill de Blasio of New York City announced the largest community school initiative in the country, connected to the largest school improvement initiative in the country.

Part of that effort included an extension of the school day by one hour, for every child in each of 94 new "Renewal" community schools. The NYC Coalition for Educational Justice (CEJ) was monitoring the city budget process to make sure that this mayoral commitment was fully funded, and discovered that funding had not been included in the budget to cover the costs of staffing for the extended time.

Parents from CEJ launched an effort to pressure the administration to allocate the necessary funds, including collaborating with expanded learning time experts to calculate the funds needed for the initiative, and planning press conferences to bring public attention to the issue. After a month of intense pressure from CEJ parents, the city agreed to commit $26 million for all 94 schools to pay school staff for additional work hours—allowing schools to start the school year with the additional resources necessary to enhance instruction. This funding has continued in subsequent years.

During the course of developing its campaign for college-ready community schools, a team of CEJ parents visited Cincinnati to learn about their community schools initiative. One of the lessons that Cincinnati community school leaders stressed was the importance of having a simple district policy that defines the essential components of a community school, so that community schools become a part of permanent district policy, rather than the pet project of a single political administration.

The following year, as the New York City Department of Education (NYCDOE) embarked on the largest community schools initiative in the country, CEJ leaders urged the city to develop its own community schools policy. Parent leaders conducted research on policies in other cities, drafted a NYC policy, collected feedback from several dozen community school partner organizations to improve it, and then released the policy at a press conference with ally organizations, urging the city to adopt it as official policy.

When, after six months and many more meetings the city had not moved forward, CEJ and its allies embarked on a series of public events to increase pressure on the administration. This resulted in the NYCDOE revising and proposing the policy to its governance board, which adopted the official NYC Community Schools Policy in January 2016. CEJ then developed a parent-friendly, bilingual version of the policy and distributed to tens of thousands of community school parents.

These are two instances in which advocacy from parents who are deeply committed to community schools succeeded in delivering significant funds and policy infrastructure to community schools, without which the schools' success and sustainability would have been severely compromised. Strong parent advocates are an insurance policy against the inevitable changes in funding streams, political leaders, and other dynamics outside of a school's control.

Funding, Staffing, and Sustaining Transformative Family Engagement

Building and sustaining transformative parent engagement in community schools requires constant tending, especially because parents are always circulating in and out of the school, and their availability for school leadership changes as their own life circumstances change. Some possibilities for staffing based on our experiences in New York include:

- CBO-level: Many lead partner CBOs hire a staff person, or an Ameri-Corps/VISTA worker, to focus exclusively on parent and community engagement. It is important that this person receive training in research-based methods of parent engagement, and the support necessary to change school practices. This position is paid for out of grants from the city, state, and federal-level, and/or private funding.
- School-level: In New York City and several other cities, schools are required to have a Parent Coordinator or another position who is responsible for supporting parent engagement in the school. This position is paid for by district tax-levy dollars.
- District-level: In New York City, the DOE's Office of Community Schools maintains a team of Parent Outreach Specialists who coach community school and CBO staff in effective methods of parent outreach and parent engagement. They support schools with outreach for parent-teacher conferences, organizing community forums, and hold training for parents on a variety of topics. This team is paid for by a combination of district tax-levy dollars, state and federal community school funds. New York City's Office of Community Schools also pro-

vides the city's 225 community schools with a wide range of resources regarding family engagement, including support with implementation of models like Academic Parent Teacher Teams and Parent-Teacher Home Visits (New York City Department of Education, n.d.).

- Other schools partner or contract with parent leadership organizations such as the Parent-Teacher Home Visit Project or the Parent Engagement Institute to guide parent engagement inside their schools, and support it through the school budget or foundation grants.
- Community organizing coalitions like the NYC Coalition for Educational Justice (CEJ) are composed of neighborhood-based advocacy groups that partner with their local schools to bring in additional programs and resources. Those advocacy groups are generally supported by foundation grants. CEJ has created a parent training curriculum that includes topics such as: What is a community school; Transformative parent engagement; Outreach and base-building; Communications and public speaking; and Holding an effective meeting. That curriculum is publicly accessible and can be modified by any school or organization.[13] Other examples are statewide coalitions like the Alliance for Quality Education, which has been pivotal in achieving increased funding for public schools, and national coalitions like Journey for Justice, which has fought to stop school closings and privatization, and to allow struggling schools to become community schools.
- Parent-level: Some schools hire parents part- or full-time to lead this area of work. There needs to be ongoing training of parent leaders, as well as staff guidance and supervision. This position can be paid for by Title 1 parent engagement funds, or community school grants.

FINAL THOUGHTS

Most of us have been in schools where staff, community organizations, and parent leaders have a vision of a true partnership school, but are frustrated by the challenges of building deep and sustained family engagement. Often, they are using ineffective techniques year after year, hoping for different results, and then getting discouraged. They blame families, or blame themselves, for the limited parent engagement, without an awareness of the methods and techniques that could help them actually achieve their vision.

Implementing transformative parent engagement isn't easy or quick. It is a labor-intensive process of building trust, developing relationships, practicing self-reflection and self-criticism, listening to and incorporating multiple perspectives, stretching outside one's comfort zone, and changing entrenched practices. Transformative parent engagement requires school staff to rethink deeply held assumptions, reconfigure basic modes of interaction, and realign the flow of power.

But that is exactly the work of building a community school. Without those careful, probing, uncomfortable processes, a community school is just a school that houses a variety of programs and services, but will never be a true partnership between school and community, and will not live up to the full vision of the community schools strategy (Valli, Stefanski, & Jacobson, 2014).

While family engagement will look different at every school, every school can build strong family engagement by using research-based methods and dedicating sufficient staff time to the work. The investment may be bigger than many schools expect, but the payoff for the school, families, and students can take a school to new horizons.

REFERENCES

A+ NYC. (n.d.). Whole child, whole school, whole city: An education roadmap for the next mayor. Retrieved from http://schottfoundation.org/sites/default /files/resources/aplusnyc-whole-child-whole-city-whole-city.pdf.

Anderson, M. D. (2016, November 15). Stereotypes are at the heart of parent-teacher communication. Retrieved October 1, 2018, from https://www .theatlantic.com/education/archive/2016/11/which-parents-are-teachers-most -likely-to-contact/507755/.

Aronson, B., and Laugnter, J. (2016, March). The theory and practice of culturally relevant education: A synthesis of research across content areas. *Review of Education Research, 86*(1), 163–206.

Bryk, A. S., & Schneider, B. L. (2002). *Trust in schools: A core resource for improvement*. New York: Russell Sage Foundation.

Bryk, A. S., Sebring, P. B., Allensworth, E., Easton, J. Q., & Luppescu, S. (2010). *Organizing schools for improvement lessons from Chicago*. Chicago: University of Chicago Press.

Capers, N., & Shah, S. C. (2015). The power of community schools. *Voices in Urban Education, 40*, 27–35.

Epstein, J. L., & Sheldon, S. B. (2002). Present and accounted for: Improving student attendance through family and community involvement. *Journal of Educational Research, 95*, 308–318.

Fletcher, M. (2016). Making space for collaboration and leadership: The role of program staff in successful family engagement initiatives. *Voices in Urban Education, 44*. Retrieved from http://vue.annenberginstitute.org/issues/44 /making-space-collaboration-and-leadership-role-program-staff-successful -family-engagemen-0.

Gershenson, S., Holt, S. B., & Papageorge, N. (2015). Who believes in me? The effect of student teacher demographic match on teacher expectations (W.E. Upjohn Institute working paper). Kalamazoo, MI: Upjohn Institute for Employment Research. Retrieved from https://research.upjohn.org/up_working papers/231/.

Gershenson, S., & Papageorge, N. (2017). The power of teacher expectations: How racial bias hinders student attainment. *Education Next, 18*(1). Retrieved from https://www.educationnext.org/power-of-teacher-expectations-racial -bias-hinders-student-attainment/.

Goff, P. A., Jackson, M. C., Di Leone, B. A. L., Culotta, C. M., & Ditomasso, N. A. (2014). The essence of innocence: Consequences of dehumanizing black children. *Journal of Personality and Social Psychology, 106*(4), 526–545. https://doi.org/10.1037/a0035663.

Henderson, A. T., & Mapp, K. L. (2002). *A new wave of evidence: The impact of school, family, and community connections on student achievement.* Austin, TX: National Center for Family & Community Connections with Schools: Southwest Educational Development Laboratory.

New York City Department of Education. (n.d.). Family engagement. Retrieved from http://www.communityschools.nyc/home/families.

Parker, C. B. (2015, April 15). Teachers more likely to label black students as troublemakers, Stanford research shows. Retrieved October 2, 2018, from https://news.stanford.edu/2015/04/15/discipline-black-students-041515/.

Sangha, S. (2013, March 22). Public school supporters seek to shape New York City education policy. *The New York Times.* Retrieved from https://www .nytimes.com/2013/03/24/nyregion/public-school-supporters-seek-to-shape -new-york-city-education-policy.html.

Stefanski, A., Valli, L., & Jacobson, R. (2016). Beyond involvement and engage- ment: The role of the family in school-community partnerships. *School Com- munity Journal, 26*(2), 135–160.

U.S. Department of Education. (2016). *The state of racial diversity in the educator workforce*. Retrieved from https://www2.ed.gov/rschstat/eval/highered /racial-diversity/state-racial-diversity-workforce.pdf.

Valli, L., Stefanski, A., & Jacobson, R. (2014). Typologizing school–community partnerships: A framework for analysis and action. *Urban Education*.

Westmoreland, H., Rosenberg, H. M., Lopez, M. E., & Weiss, H. (2009). Seeing is believing: Promising practices for how school districts promote family engagement (issue brief). Cambridge, MA: Harvard Family Research Project and Chicago, IL: PTA.

Westrich, L. and Strobel, K. (2013). *A study of family engagement in Redwood City community schools*. Stanford, CA: John W. Gardner Center for Youth and their Communities.

Chapter Seven

Voices for Equity

Youth Leadership in Oakland Community Schools

Kendra Fehrer and Aurora Lopez[1]

If you have come here to help me, you are wasting your time. But if you have come because your liberation is bound up with mine, then let us work together.

—Lilla Watson

While over the last decades youth have come to play an increasingly important role as researchers, planners, advocates, evaluators, and decision makers in nonprofit organizations and other community institutions, K–12 schools as a whole have been noticeably absent from this arena (Cervone & Cushman, 2002). Schools face many barriers to meaningful youth participation, including entrenched hierarchies, rigid bureaucratic systems, and embedded cultural attitudes that prescribe the role of students and adults (Shah & Mediratta, 2008). Especially in high-poverty schools, youth face tremendous obstacles to school engagement and success. In many schools, students are perceived as unmotivated, apathetic, or, worse, disruptors that need to be controlled (Warren, Mira, and Nikundiwe, 2008).

Most proponents of community schools would argue that the approach envisions a different experience for youth. By providing integrated student supports, opportunities for expanded learning, and meaningful family engagement, community schools aim to generate a truly student-centered environment that supports the development of the "whole child." (Dryfoos, 2005).

Integrated student supports help youth build strength and resilience, allowing them to come to class better ready to learn. Academic and enrichment expanded learning programs allow youth to develop competence, a sense of belonging, connections with a caring adult, and contribute to their community in meaningful ways. And intentional strategies to engage parents in the school community help to align arguably two of the most important spheres in a child's life: home and school. These services, supports, and opportunities can provide young people with important developmental assets and protective factors they need to become healthy and successful adults.[2]

Yet youth have important roles to play in their educational success beyond simply being recipients of services and programs to help them thrive (Warren et al., 2008). Positive youth development research has well established that opportunities for meaningful participation help youth develop skills and competencies they need to become healthy adults and successful learners (McLaughlin, 2000; Eccles & Gootman, 2002; Salusky, Larson, Griffith, Wu, Raffaelli, Sugimura, & Guzman, 2014).

However, beyond these developmental outcomes, youth participation can also be a powerful force for social change—transforming the very institutional norms and power relations that engender youth disengagement and alienation in the first place (Warren et al., 2008; Kirshner, 2015; Ginwright & James, 2002; Cervone & Cushman, 2002).

As the main "receivers" of education, youth have indispensable insight on what works, what doesn't, and what can be done to improve all aspects of their school experience. When youth move from receivers of education to engaged partners, students develop an increased sense of ownership over their school community and academic success, often leading to an improved view of education and greater academic engagement (important conditions for student success).

Beyond supporting individual student outcomes, this kind of engagement also shifts the culture of the school community and system. By placing value on students as "experts," we can transform the educational system from one that is often transactional and alienating, to one of meaningful engagement and partnership.

While youth around the country and world have demonstrated their potential to enact meaningful educational change, what they cannot do on their own is "create the climate and conditions that will permit them to take these participatory roles in society on a widespread scale. That is the challenge and the task of the adult world" (National Commission on Youth Development, 1975, as cited in Cervone & Cushmann, 2002). So to what extent are adults in community schools creating conditions for meaningful youth participation? How are youth and adults working to shift entrenched dynamics to create new structures, beliefs, and practices around youth engagement? What would that engagement look like?

In this chapter, we explore these questions through the story of Oakland Unified School District's (OUSD) transformation into a full-service community school district and the roles that youth have played. In some ways, this is not exclusively a community school story: Oakland youth were involved as powerful actors in school transformation long before the district made its commitment to embrace community schools. Situating the story of youth's role in OUSD community schools within broader youth efforts for educational equity is important for multiple reasons.

First, it is the story that Oakland student activists themselves tell. The "awakening" of a social-political consciousness, of positive racial identities, and of the power of collective action to transform the circumstances and conditions of young peoples' lives undergirds young peoples' experience and the work they continue to do in Oakland schools.

Secondly, the organizing accomplished by youth in these movements developed a rich tapestry of youth-led community-based organizations in Oakland that would precipitate powerful changes to district culture and policy. The rich civic fabric of youth organizations enabled both the infrastructure and the political will for constructing a meaningful role for youth in OUSD community schools. Foregrounding this history provides important context on the political, cultural, and community conditions for meaningful youth engagement in community schools.

Lastly, situating the story of youth role in OUSD community schools within the broader lens of youth organizing highlights a critical feature of both OUSD's student engagement work and community schools initiative: an unrelenting focus on equity. In OUSD, community schools emerged as a deliberate and explicit strategy to disrupt persistent inequalities for Oakland youth. This framing echoed that of youth organizers struggling for racial and educational justice, and ties these two efforts together.

By sharing the story of Oakland community schools, youth activism, and how these two have shaped each other, we hope to shine light on the potential community schools offer to create powerful roles for young people in transforming their education. Not only do young people benefit from meaningful participation, but our civic and social institutions grow

stronger when young people can contribute their critical gaze and participate in efforts for improvement.

FOUNDATIONS: FROM "SCHOOLS NOT JAILS" TO MEANINGFUL STUDENT ENGAGEMENT

*Students are the ones sitting behind a desk every weekday in a class-
room; students are the ones receiving an education, whether it is a
quality education or not. So, why are decisions being made for students
without student input? Students should be a part of decision making
when it comes to education.*

—ACCSU Student Power Newsletter, March 25, 2014

When asked to describe the beginning of youth involvement in Oakland community schools, youth activists and district staff start the
story much further back. They begin the story in the mid-1990s, a time
of youth outrage and awakening in urban California. The year 1992
marked the quincentennial of Columbus's arrival to the Americas, spur-
ring a burst of "counter-celebrations" from indigenous and Chicano/a
community groups.

Shortly thereafter, a series of ballot measures were introduced that
would disproportionately negatively affect young people of color. In
1994, Proposition 187 passed, denying public benefits—for example,
public education and non-emergency health services—to undocumented
immigrants.[3] Latino youth in cities across the state mobilized, forming a
broad coalition articulating a platform of demands—central among these
demands was access to a quality public education.

These mobilizations would create the conditions and infrastructure for
sustained organizing by Oakland youth.[4] When Proposition 21 was introduced in 2000, proposing changes to the juvenile criminal code that would
result in significantly harsher sentences for youth (and, again, disproportionately affect young people of color), youth organizers were poised to
form a new coalition. "Schools Not Jails" became a core refrain of the
movement, as youth called on lawmakers to repeal punitive criminal
justice measures and invest in under-resourced public schools. Oakland
students of color were highly mobilized, organizing demonstrations in the

state's capital with thousands of their peers, shutting down schools and freeways across the state.

At the time of these mobilizations, Oakland public schools were notorious for poor conditions—overcrowding, lack of adequate classroom supplies, crumbling infrastructure, high teacher turnover, and high levels of dropout to name a few (Kirshner, 2015; Goldwasser, 2004). These toxic educational experiences effected students largely along racial and geographic lines and were refracted in students' educational and life outcomes, including high student dropout rates, poor attendance, and disengagement.[5] Youth organizers had begun actively addressing these conditions through local mobilizations and youth leadership work in schools.

With the support of then-superintendent George Musgrove, student activists also established a district "youth steering committee," charged with interrogating the high levels of dropout and disengagement and developing recommendations for district policy to redress these issues. The committee embarked upon a large-scale action research project involving a survey of over 1,000 students, followed by multiple youth-led forums, to examine root causes of high student dropout and disengagement.

The result was a series of recommendations to the district that would facilitate youth engagement in school and district decision making, create opportunities for youth action research, and provide district infrastructure (e.g., staffing, budget, training) to support it all.[6] They called their proposal the Student Power Resolution.[7]

The board was poised to vote on the resolution when financial crisis struck, and the district was placed into state receivership. All nonessential district functions stalled, and the resolution was tabled. However, youth did not desist—they simply continued the work without the district's active participation. On top of the district budget crisis, the city was encountering financial strain, closing libraries and community resources. No Child Left Behind had recently come into effect, resulting in punitive measures for poorly performing schools. Due to the budget crisis and policy changes, many local schools were being closed or threatening to be closed.

In the face of these conditions, youth organized a massive student walk-out and a youth forum to engage their peers on the issues and their proposed solutions, articulated in the Student Power Resolution. The state-appointed administrator overseeing the district, Randy Ward, had been vocal in his refusals to field proposals from "special interests" in the community. However, to the surprise of many youth activists, Ward attended the forum and, even more surprisingly, agreed to the students' demands for district support of meaningful student engagement.

A new group—composed of many of the same organizations and individuals—was established, calling themselves the Meaningful Student Engagement (MSE) Collaborative. The collaborative included dozens of youth-led organizations across Oakland and built on the work of the Student Power Resolution to articulate a vision of what meaningful student engagement could look like as district practice. One organizer describes their approach:

> We started off with a vision of what student power looks like. We went through a process of defining it, with the frame of, "when a student takes a leadership class, what are the outcomes we're aiming for? How should a student be after taking leadership? Individually, what does that look like? At the school site level, what would be true, would that look like, if we had meaningful student engagement?" We started with a brainstorm and visioning session, then narrowed it down to a few bullets. It took us about a year to do it. Simultaneously, what we were also doing, once we drafted the standards, we also drafted a curriculum for a class. Every youth-based organization or group involved brought their [leadership/youth development] curriculum. We went through all the curriculums, flagged what fit where. We came up with Standards, then an outline for the curriculum. If a student should have knowledge of self, what curriculum do we have that gets at that? We had about 18–22 organizations involved. While the group got smaller over time, we always had at least 11 core organizations, with more contributing organizations.

In essence, the MSE Standards represented a complete re-visioning of student participation in schools, and outlined a student-power, equity-centered vision of student leadership. Youth were expected to take ownership of their own education, develop an analysis of power and oppression, commit to serving *all* students (not just specific individuals or groups), and use research and critical thinking to develop solutions to problems. Adults were expected to support the conditions for meaningful student engagement. This included ensuring a budget for student leadership development, facilitating student access to decision makers (e.g., offer regular meetings with principal and other administrators to dialogue about student concerns), and encouraging non-traditional leaders.

The standards also outlined structural and systemic supports needed to facilitate youth leadership. Under the MSE Standards, all students would have access to leadership classes in school. There would be a district-wide student advisory body. There would be a staff position, a website, and training provided to adults in what it means to work in partnership with young people in an education setting. A curriculum would be rolled out to all high schools and middle schools to support students and adults with what it means to fulfill the Standards. (For complete MSE Standards and Student Bill of Rights, see Appendixes A and B.)

In April 2007, at the recommendation of the Meaningful Student Engagement Collaborative and other youth and community advocates in Oakland, the OUSD Board of Education adopted the MSE Standards.[8]

Taken together, these standards completely rewrote the traditional role of youth in educational institutions. They demonstrated an emphasis on equity and inclusion of under-represented students and of students as essential stakeholders in educational decision-making processes. They underscored the responsibility not only of student leaders, but also the institutions themselves in creating structures and opportunities for youth's meaningful engagement. And they designated funding for a district staff position to implement the work that the district would undertake in operationalizing the Standards.[9]

While some districts have made strides to include youth representation in district governance—for example, including youth positions on a school board or supporting youth advisory committees—to our knowledge, these standards are unique in a U.S. school district context. (They are also among the most long-lived; the 2017–2018 academic year marks 10 years since the district's adoption of the MSE standards, and the youth engagement work is still going strong.)

These earlier years of youth organizing in Oakland and the eventual creation of the MSE Standards are critical elements of Oakland's community school story. Not only did they lay the groundwork for an expanded role for youth in OUSD community schools, but they also helped catalyze and shape the community school initiative itself.

BECOMING A COMMUNITY SCHOOL DISTRICT: STUDENT SUPPORTS, QUALITY TEACHING, AND POSITIVE CULTURE/CLIMATE

All City Council (ACC) is a student union, led by students, working with Oakland Unified School District (OUSD) to create the necessary changes in Oakland schools that will benefit the students of Oakland, and the community. All City Council Student Union (ACCSU) has a general campaign that is called "Making A-G real." This campaign has three pillars which are Student Support, Quality Teaching and Safety, from which ACC's yearly campaign focus is based. ACCSU has a vision that each and every student attending an Oakland public school will be adequately prepared for life after high school, whether it be college life or a career life. ACCSU envisions that each and every student will have the necessary tools to make it through high school and fulfill their full potential. Who else can represent student voice better than a student, better yet nine students; ACCSU has a governing board consisting of nine students attending various Oakland public high schools. Two of these governing board members have a seat on the Board of Education. To ensure that we are capturing the voices of the students attending Oakland public schools, ACCSU hosts a general meeting with a different high school and middle school in OUSD every month.

—ACCSU's Student Power Newsletter, March 25, 2014

One of the primary vehicles for youth engagement in district policy was the All City Council Student Union (ACCSU). Representatives from the ACCSU governing board had participated in the Meaningful Student Engagement Collaborative. Upon the adoption of the MSE Standards, the youth representatives went back to ACCSU's governing board and, together with their peers, created a new mission, vision, and revised constitution that reflected the principals of the MSE.

The revamped ACCSU built into their structure a yearly cycle of action. Youth would conduct research with their peers across the district, focus on a particular issue widely and deeply felt, then engage with their peers and adults to deliberate possible solutions, and make policy recommendations or participate in advocacy if needed.

In 2007/2008, the ACCSU annual campaign had focused on youths' deep concerns with student dropout. As youth activists looked into the

root causes of student dropout, they found that OUSD high school graduation requirements were not aligned with the California public UC and
State University system's A-G requirements. As a result, many low-
income students of color were graduating from high school ill-prepared
and ineligible for admittance to the state's public university system.

Youth called for a complete overhaul of the graduation requirements, in
a campaigned that became known as "Making A-G Real." As a result of
students' advocacy, the district changed its policy so that all high schools'
graduation requirements now reflect the state's A-G requirements.

While changing the graduation requirements was a critical victory
and necessary improvement, student advocates realized that changing
the graduation policy was not sufficient to ensure all students graduated
college-ready. As one youth organizer stated: "If students don't have
support—like tutoring, health care, transportation—if they don't have
a safe, positive school culture and climate, and if they don't have quality teachers, they can't be successful in preparing for college, career,
and life."

Out of youths' action research and analysis arose the three pillars of
the A-G campaign: Student Supports, Quality Teaching, and Safety and
Positive Culture/Climate. While the ACCSU has gone through multiple
cycles of inquiry, these three pillars remain at the core of their work. They
also would become widely felt priorities among youth and adults alike as
the district explored setting a new course upon regaining local control.

When the district gained local control in 2009, after nearly six years of
state receivership, then-superintendent Tony Smith embarked upon a listening campaign to help determine the future direction of the district. As
part of the listening campaign, Smith's administration established thirteen
task forces, each involving student and community input, covering topics
ranging from African American male achievement, to literacy, to school
finances and budgeting, to principal leadership. Youth voice was critical
in this process, informing broad concerns that youth had articulated based
on previous organizing and cycles of inquiry.

The newly hired district youth engagement coordinator (an OUSD
alumna and former student organizer herself) facilitated youth involvement in this process. Youth participated in nearly all of the committees
and played an especially formative role in the culture/climate and secondary school committees.

Some of the task force recommendations included specific recommendations generated by youth action research, especially in the areas of student supports; for example, peer-to-peer academic counseling, social-emotional supports for students (which later became a call for social-emotional learning standards in the district), ethnic studies, and restorative justice practices. At this time, the MSE Standards were also readopted into the district's strategic vision, to make sure they "lived" within community schools.[10]

Community schools emerged as the lynchpin to hold these multifaceted strategies together. Youth had played a role in determining the priorities community schools sought to address. They had already shown their effectiveness at informing district strategy (i.e., changing graduation requirement policy). And they firmly felt the community school vision reflected their own voices and needs.

Since 2010, OUSD has been transforming its schools into community schools. The initiative has sustained and grown over the course of five superintendents. As of the 2017–2018 academic year, 35 of Oakland's 86 district-run schools are community schools.[11] This includes the majority of OUSD high schools, as well as an increasing number of elementary and middle school community schools.[12]

OUSD community schools provide students with a range of opportunities and supports, including school-based health centers, behavioral health initiatives (e.g., positive behavioral intervention and support, restorative justice, attendance and discipline support services), social-emotional learning, after-school and summer learning programs, and student and family engagement.[13] While each OUSD community school varies in the way they have adapted the approach, several core practices and strategies define Oakland community schools.

At a mature OUSD community school, a visitor will often see partner- and school-based staff working to provide *culturally responsive services and supports* to students and their families aligned with specific student and school goals—for example, a restorative justice program aimed to address disproportionate suspensions or after-school programs that "push in" to the classroom.

Principals practice *distributed leadership*, including the community school manager (CSM), as a high-level administrator, and leveraging opportunities to engage parents in school decision making and improvement. One also finds high-functioning *collaborative structures and practices* such as Coordination of Services Teams (to refer students to needed services) and attendance teams (an integrated approach to reducing chronic absence) to address students' barriers to learning. Oakland community schools draw on *strategic partnerships* with community-based organizations that actively work with school staff toward concrete and specific school goals and dynamic *data systems* that provide the school community with consistent feedback to inform decision making.[14]

While many community school resources are provided by partner organizations, they are also supported by a district department, the Department of Community Schools and Student Services (CSSS), which houses all non-academic district student, family, and community support services.

CSSS staff, in addition to securing funding for and overseeing administration of many of these areas, also provides school-level staff with ongoing professional development, training, and coaching (e.g., a professional learning community for Community School Managers); co-develop and communicate district-wide standards of practice (e.g., protocols for quality partnerships, best practices for Coordination of Services Teams), and work to align community schools efforts with other district initiative (e.g., connect site-level staff to relevant district resources, align CSSS efforts *within* the district).

These departmental activities and strategies are undergirded by a firm commitment to ensure that every OUSD community school offers each student the culturally relevant and appropriate services and opportunities they need to learn and thrive; provides a safe, supportive, and engaging environment for teaching and learning; and is staffed by adults who are culturally competent, collaborative, and actively working to redress persistent inequalities.

While a vast array of diverse organizations and constituents shaped the formation and development of Oakland's community schools initiative, at its core it reflects the concerns voiced by youth in the student organizing of the 1990s, the Student Power Resolution and the MSE Standards, and the identified in the ACCSU "Making A-G Real" campaign.

The focus on equity, leveraging partnerships to provide culturally responsive supports for students, focus on transforming school culture/

climate, and bolstering meaningful student and family engagement point back to youth voice as an important force in the shaping of OUSD community schools.

YOUTH IN OUSD COMMUNITY SCHOOLS TODAY

Oakland community schools have re-imagined youth government as a training ground for youth researchers, organizers, and advocates. School-level staff are scaffolded with curriculum and coaching to act as adult allies supporting youth leaders to address important issues at their school.[15] These efforts are bolstered by district staff, as well as a robust coalition of youth-centered community-based organizations. The youth engagement work has merged with other district efforts to facilitate greater partnership and participation across Oakland communities.

What started as the Meaningful Student Engagement initiative became the Office of Student, Family, and Community Engagement (OSFCE), and is now housed within the Department of Community Schools and Student Supports. Most of the OSFCE staff are OUSD alumni and former student leaders themselves. The OSFCE aims to "inspire, engage and support the students, families, and communities of OUSD in becoming authentic co-owners of our schools, sharing responsibility for every student becoming college and career ready."[16] The OSFCE has developed an explicit theory of action around student engagement that aligns with the youth organizing and leadership approach outlined in the MSE Standards (see Figure 7.1).

In the coming sections, we'll share in the words of youth activists and adult allies what some of the district's youth engagement initiatives look like in terms of school-site and district-level practice. These efforts are aligned with OUSD community school goals of ensuring that every school (1) offers each student culturally relevant and appropriate services and opportunities they need to learn; (2) provides a safe, supportive, and engaging environment for teaching and learning; and (3) is staffed by adults who are culturally competent, collaborative, and actively working toward equity so that each student graduates college, career, and community ready.

They also reflect national community school standards that emphasize equity, a whole child approach, building on community strengths, using

OUSD Student and Family Engagement Theory of Action

Engaging students and families to increase equity by improving school culture, student achievement and college readiness.

OUSD Engagement Goals

- Increase representation from school sites on district engagement bodies
- At School Sites, increase representation and participation of students and families from under-represented and underserved communities.
- At School Sites, establish shared governance bodies in compliance with LCFF, MSFE Standards, Core Waiver
- At School Sites, engage more students and families from under-represented/underserved communities in school improvement efforts.
- Align school-led and CBO-led engagement efforts at school sites, towards mutual school improvement goals.

Engagement Pyramid

Level 4) Get involved in DISTRICT-level Engagement

District Engagement Activities

- LCAP Parent Advisory, LCAP ELL Parent Advisory
- Student Directors on Board of Education (advisory vote)
- LCAP Student Advisory
- ACC Governing Board

- Shared decision-making
- Advise LCAP priorities and implementation in the district.
- Provide representative leadership for your site and constituency and bring info back to respective school sites

Students/Parents move to Level 4

Level 3) Get involved in SCHOOL governance

District Engagement Activities

- PR the BAR monthly trainings for School Governance Teams (prep for SGT/SSC Summits)
- SPED Parent Summit

- Shared decision-making
- Ensure stakeholder priorities are implemented
- Set budget priorities
- Evaluate impact

Site Engagement Activities

- School Governance Team (SGT)
- LCAP Cttes: African-American Parent Council, ELL Parent Ctte, SPED Parent Advisory
- MSFE Committee
- Classroom Observations

Students/Parents move to Level 3

Level 2) Get involved to help your SCHOOL improve

District Engagement Activities

- ACC Middle and High School mtgs/trainings
- Middle and High School Peer Resources/Eth Studies Conferences
- Youth Leadership Summit

- Understand school data
- Help set and implement school improvement priorities
- Provide input on school policy and practice, and feedback for school staff
- Opportunities for all families to engage with learning and volunteering
- Leadership Dvlpt programs for students
- Leadership Dvlpt programs for parents/families

Site Engagement Activities

- RJ Peer leaders
- CBO engagement events
- Elections for SGT and LCAP Cttes
- MSFE Student/Family Forums
- Elections of Student Officers
- Parent Volunteers with attendance, culture, reading
- Academic Parent-Teacher Teams
- Peer mentors/educators

Students/Parents move to Level 2

Level 1) Get informed to help your CHILD succeed

District Engagement Activities

- Common Core Workshops
- LCAP input events

- Learn about academies, internships and other opportunities
- Learn to navigate school
- Learn about Common Core
- Parent-Teacher Communication
- Address student/parent complaints
- Parent support programs
- Info translated, and accessible mtg locations/times
- Welcoming School Environment
- Student Leadership and Civic Engagement classes class
- Student support service programs

Site Engagement Activities

- Back to School Night
- Parent Orientations
- Family Resource Centers
- Parent Skills Trainings
- Mailings/Calls

Point of Entry - for Parents/Families and Students to get involved

Figure 7.1. OUSD Student and Family Engagement Theory of Action

Source: https://www.ousd.org/Page/11996

data and community wisdom, commitment to interdependence, investment in trusting relationships, and building a learning organization.[17]
While youth and adult allies in Oakland are among the first to say that
there is much work still to be done, the school-level and district-level
practices described here are a critical ingredient to successful community
school implementation.

SCHOOL-LEVEL YOUTH ENGAGEMENT: MIDDLE SCHOOL YOUTH ORGANIZE TO IMPROVE SCHOOL NUTRITION

*The middle school division of ACCSU works on enhancing their al-
ready strong leadership skills. ACCSU works with middle students to
think about present issues at their school and what is best for their
school as a whole. After accessing the voices of the student body and
looking at the root causes for this issue, each leadership class will create an action project that address an existing problem at their school
such as bullying, student bonding or culture sensitivity. The way they
frame and build their project is left for the student leaders to decide
but ACCSU gives each school's student leaders the tools they need to
complete their projects and are there for additional support. Upon the
completion of these projects, each school will be expected to present
about their project at the end of the year celebration for All City Council's middle school division. In these presentations, they will talk about
the issue their project addressed and the outcome of the project. Each
school will also be presenting on how they hope that their project will
live on and evolve as time goes on. Everything done in middle school
ACCSU is preparing the middle school leaders for high school part
of ACCSU and to get them excited about leadership and high school.*

—ACCSU's Student Power Newsletter, March 25, 2014

In this section we focus on the experience of youth leaders and their adult
allies at a middle school in East Oakland who have been working to improve
school nutrition. The leadership coordinator has been supporting students in
this work for the last five years in this work. All OUSD high schools have a
similar leadership coordinator, as do many of its middle schools.

The leadership coordinators are typically teachers, who take on the role
in addition to their primary instructional duties. The leadership coordina-

tors are supported by district training, ongoing coaching, or consulting with central office student engagement staff (and occasionally other youth leaders or adult allies from partner organizations), and an extensive handbook outlining roles, expectations, philosophy, curriculum, and more. As our middle school leadership coordinator described:

> When I got the binder that they give us for this program, I really saw the lens that Oakland has around leadership. Not just teachers hand-picking the "good students," but finding students with potential, maybe not the grades, but the leadership ability who can represent their school, give back to their school. Over the years, I've been able to inspire a lot of student leaders. Generally, for each grade there is a president, a vice president, a secretary, a treasurer, and two independents. There are typically anywhere from 25–30 students in leadership.

Student leaders participate in weekly leadership classes and activities, either at lunch and/or after-school. Importantly, student leaders are not necessarily the 4.0 students with the stellar school records, but rather, students with potential to make a difference. Student leaders are elected by their peers, in a fairly typical school election process. Interested students are encouraged to sign up during lunchtime.

The leadership coordinator calls a meeting to explain the campaign process and what it means to be a student leader in OUSD. Students then have a week to campaign before elections. The day before voting, students have a chance to address their peers in speeches. After election day, votes are tallied, and usually within the next 36 hours, winners are announced. However, unlike conventional student governments, once elected, students must review and sign a contract outlining their duties as student leaders as defined in the MSE Standards.[18]

One of the cornerstones of student leadership in OUSD is the school improvement project, usually embedded within a participant action research cycle. At the school we describe here, students have been working to implement improvements in school nutrition. In the words of the adult ally/leadership coordinator:

> The idea came from the students themselves. In the leadership program, they have to identify a problem at their school and come up with a way to solve it. We did a brainstorm about problems at the school. Lunch was one of the things that resonated with everyone. What they told me was the lunch

was often inedible. It gets you sick. You don't want to eat it. Staff have said they eat it and get sick. Students were frustrated with it. If you don't feed a student something good and wholesome, behavior issues are going to increase. It's also going to help them be better at home, if they're well-fed.

So the first time we worked on this was 2 years ago. The food and lunch lady were horrible. We scheduled a meeting with the head of the nutritional department at the district. I was out sick the day of the meeting, so I had one of the other staff come and help. They asked the students, "So, what do you think we could do?" So the district made some adjustments and we got a new lunch lady. She shifted things. Her son was an 8th grader at the school. She wanted to be there. She put a lot of love in the food. Then, she was promoted. And the problem came back.

So now, we're doing more work. The students did some research and found out that the food comes from the district, and is from the same company that serves food in prisons. The kids were really hurt by this. So they're now out surveying their peers. Once we have this data next year, we'll see if the district will at least open up the snack bar for the rest of the year. Otherwise, students are going to go to the newspapers. The district needs to see that we're serious.

The role of the adult ally in this process is to support the students as they drive the work forward. As described above, the improvement project involves identifying an issue that is important to the student body at large, conducting research on "the problem," consulting with peers as needed, meeting with their principal to discuss the issue and the findings of their research, and proposing institutional and systemic changes to address the problem.

As a result of students' work to improve nutrition services at multiple schools, youth are now part of the district's central office nutritional services committee, providing ongoing feedback and recommendations to support better school nutrition at schools across the district.

For adults used to working in schools in other capacities, for example, as teachers or administrators, stepping into the role of leadership coordinator and adult ally can be challenging, as learning to be a skillful adult ally is a process—especially as it requires shifting the traditional teacher–student relationship found in most schools. As one teacher reflects:

Over the years, I've learned to step back and give the students full autonomy. Take my hands out of the pot, and truly just facilitate. Like with meetings. I usually came around and would look for them to remind them. But I stopped doing it. "It's your thing. You need to have your voice." Also, in terms of picking things to do, brainstorming. I used to sway the process, but I don't do that anymore. I used to drive the committees, I feel like I had more of the hands-on approach, you need to do this, you need to do that. I've learned to shift my approach, more like say, "Hey, we've already established some things. These are the tools you have to create that." More like asking questions, letting them explore the process. I may provide an outline of what we do, but really am giving them a lot of control.

Additionally, becoming an adult ally includes overcoming many of the mind-sets adults hold about authority, "acceptable" youth behavior, and meaningful change. As one teacher put it, it means acknowledging that "our students aren't disrespectful because they advocate for what they need. If they disagree with you appropriately, what is the problem? You have to hear what they say. You need to have a conversation." Also, adults may struggle to redefine *who* can be seen as a student leader. As one teacher stated,

Not all the teachers understand. They'll say, "You need to get him out of the program because he cut class." Shifting that idea, away from the punitive towards seeing the potential. . . . I've had some experience with . . . the rigidity of certain mind-sets, how students should and shouldn't act, what a leader should look like.

Shifting this view of who can be a leader is tremendously important, as youth who are most disenfranchised and disengaged often have the most to say about what's not working and what could be better (Kirshner, 2015).

Returning to our middle school leadership coordinator, she smiles as she describes how among her school's staff the culture has been shifting. The community school manager has been a strong ally, from providing operational support for youth leadership activities to being a voice for youth inclusion in school administrative meetings. The school administrative leadership has been supportive. More and more, other adult staff are identifying opportunities for student leaders to step up and play meaningful roles in school governance and decision making.

For example, just over a year ago the school was one of several invited to participate in an extensive school redesign effort initiated by the superintendent's office. Over the course of the year, youth actively participated in the process, which resulted in a lengthy proposal outlining multiple areas of school change.

As one leadership teacher stated: "Now for the most part, people recognize the students as leaders and recognize them in that position. Not everybody, but something like 80 percent. There are just a few who say, '[students] shouldn't be doing it.' But once you explain, they get it." For this teacher, being a leadership coordinator has been a much-needed breath of fresh air and has kept her going when she was on the verge of burnout. "Leadership gave me a reason to come. I was ready not to be here. If it weren't for leadership, I wouldn't be here."

While not all district middle schools have active leadership coordinators, the district office is working to train more school-site staff, including community school managers, to take on the role of adult ally. This would be especially valuable to provide extra support around student participation in not only student government and site-level action campaigns, but also school site council and Local Control Accountability Plan (LCAP), which essentially define the goals, actions, services, and expenditures that support positive student outcomes.[19]

YOUTH VOICE IN DISTRICT POLICY: CHANGING CREDIT RECOVERY POLICY SO ALL STUDENTS CAN GRADUATE

All City Council Student Union (ACCSU) seeks to create positive change in our schools. We amplify student voice by serving as a bridge between adult decision-makers and the student body. We are a diverse team of student leaders who represent or are elected by the masses of students at our schools. ACCSU organizes campaigns and activities to serve the assessed needs of our constituents; including addressing internalized, interpersonal, and institutional oppression in our daily lives and the daily functioning of our schools and working towards solutions.

We envision: (1) A strong, unified All City Council with open and constant communication with the student body, that functions as a powerful student union. ACCSU has the power to make its voice heard on all issues that impact students and is supported by an Office of Student Engagement with its own space, website, and budget. (2) Schools where student's outlook on school is transformed by engaging in leadership. Students get the support and classes they need from the District, administration, teachers, parents, and community to be job-ready and college-ready, artistically expressive, leaders, and role models. (3) A District where students are involved in decision-making on policies relating to all issues impacting students (such as budget, buildings and grounds, curriculum, discipline, etc.) and sit on hiring panels. (4) A District where leadership has a formal place during the school-day as well as in a multitude of quality after-school and community-based programs where many students participate in improving their schools and communities.

—ACCSU Mission & Vision Statement, 2014

One of the primary mechanisms for youth voice at the district-level is All City Council Student Union (ACCSU). Since the establishment of the MSE Standards and the first years of the A-G campaign, the ACCSU has tackled many issues to strengthen student supports, quality teaching, and safe culture/climate. This focus was flexible, adapting to changes in policy context to remain relevant: for example, when the California Department of Education (CDE) introduced LCAP, a new local accountability and planning structure, ACCSU's action project focused on aligning youth recommendations with LCAP goals.[20]

Similar to its school-level student leadership counterparts, ACCSU is built around an annual cycle of action. As the OUSD Youth Engagement Coordinator describes:

We start each year with a fall retreat, during which the youth revisit the accomplishments, strengths and lessons learned from the prior year. We usually come to that retreat with data on all the major topics and findings that emerged from the youth action research as well as the recommendations that were presented the year before. The retreat is attended by student organizers from throughout Oakland (not just leaders from student government), who are working on a wide range of issues that impact young people: gentrification, food justice, violence prevention. They don't bring their agenda, but they are knowledgeable in those areas. We ask them to bring any data that they have, along with what they're working on, and we also review what we did last year. It's all framed under the Making A-G Real campaign—student supports, quality teachers, safe culture/climate. At that point, the youth decide if they want to continue with the same topic, maybe a different angle, or completely switch gears. The deciding point comes after assessing the data, the climate and opportunity at the time within the school district, and the criteria: (1) is it real improvement leading to real change? (2) is it responding to current conditions? (3) does it promote social justice? (4) is there a clear target? (5) does it shifts power to students? (6) is it winnable? And lastly, (7) is this issue widely and deeply felt by students? Each individual young person at the retreat participates in a ranked vote. The proposal with the most votes determines the focus of the year.

After the youth determine their focus for the year, the team dedicates the fall for training—anything related to the campaign focus content area, research methodology, and anticipated campaign activities. Midyear, they have another retreat to assess the training from the fall and plan for the spring. In the late winter/spring, the group focuses on research, advocacy, and campaign activities. By mid to late spring, they are ready to start drafting recommendations. At the end of May, the youth present their action research findings and recommendations to the school board and ask for a pledge of support.

In 2016–2017, the previous year's inquiry had indicated that lack of effective credit recovery opportunities was a major barrier to students' graduating high school college-ready. Student leaders had learned that credit recovery programs and supports in the district were under-funded, and there were few opportunities to support ninth and tenth graders; most credit recovery supports (such as summer school) were targeted at and prioritized twelfth graders.

However, ACCSU's review of the data showed that a disturbing percentage of ninth and tenth graders were already showing as missing 10–30 percent of needed credits. While some OUSD schools were doing well in supporting students being on-track with credits, outcomes across sites were uneven. In the words of one ACCSU participant,

> There is no district policy to say how all schools should implement credit recovery. It's up to the sites. There are great things happening in some schools, but not others. So we're talking about access. Who has access to these opportunities? How do we get a school that has 90 percent graduation rate, and others have 30 percent or 40 percent?

Over the course of the fall, youth leaders reached out to district staff to invite presentations at the ACCSU general meeting. Over the course of several meetings, high-level district staff participated in these meetings, including adult staff from the office of Academic Recovery and Post-Secondary Readiness, Community Schools and Student Services, and Communications.

Students asked questions, refined their recommendations, and, ultimately, were formally invited by the school board vice president to draft a policy on credit recovery for OUSD. Over the subsequent months, the ACCSU pursued three strategies: raising awareness of credit recovery with their peers and adults; conducting further cycles of action research to garner student input, including focus groups and surveys; and dialoguing with youth and staff in other districts across the Bay Area to understand how other places were handling credit recovery supports.

In May 2017, youth leaders created their recommendations and drafted policy language. On June 28, 2017, the school board adopted Resolution 1617-0228 to Increase Graduation Rates and Strengthen Student Access to A-G Completion Through the Implementation of the Student Equity Credit Recovery and Prevention Program. The resolution included findings from the youth action research on the current status of credit recovery, and provided for an implementation team to be created in the 2017–2018 school year to develop a detailed plan and budget for the Student Equity Credit Recovery and Prevention Program, to be implemented in the 2018–2019 academic year.[21] According to the resolution document,

> The program will include among other things: Every student having access to their transcripts, communication and support plans, student access to a comprehensive list of credit recovery options available and a core list to support different learners, sustainable resources, funding or otherwise, to support the implementation of this policy by the first day of school in 2018–19. In addition the plan will include a training process and curriculum, development of training and resources for prevention and intervention strategies relating to credit recovery, and identification of staff responsibilities in plan implementation.

In sum, a youth-driven collaboration between student leaders and district staff resulted in a poignant resolution to begin to redress one of the most pressing equity issues in Oakland: inadequate access to credit recovery and subsequent high school completion. In contrast to conventional adult-driven efforts to inform or consult with students on educational decisions, the credit recovery resolution represented a youth-driven process, in which adults were engaged as allies and equal partners, to take important steps to support equity (see figure 7.2 for visualization of youth participation).[22]

They also reflect core community school standards: emphasis on equity, building on community strengths, using data and community wisdom, investment in trusting relationships, and building a learning organization. In the case described above, youth leveraged their strengths to critically analyze data and engage with their peers and high-level district staff (with whom they had built trusting relationships) to foster critical reflection, learning, and ultimately, organizational improvement.

Youth leaders have also been engaged in supporting community school goals (i.e., student supports, quality teaching, and positive culture/climate) in other ways. For example, recognizing the importance of teach-

8. Youth/Adult Equity

7. Completely Youth-Driven

6. Youth/Adult Equality

5. Youth Consulted

4. Youth Informed

3. Tokenism

2. Decoration

1. Manipulation

Figure 7.2. Ladder of Youth Voice
Source: https://freechild.org/ladder-of-youth-participation/

ers and the student–teacher relationships in student success, youth leaders have made an effort to include youth experience in OUSD teacher professional development.

In 2015–2016 youth were part of the district's orientation retreat for new teachers, where they had an opportunity to provide teachers with training from a youth perspective about what it means to walk into Oakland schools, what it means to be a strong teacher, and how to build relationships with students. Additionally, in the district's 2016–2017 search for a new superintendent, ACCSU initiated a proposal for incorporating youth voice into the hiring process, which they presented to the school board soon after the former superintendent announced his resignation.

In the proposal, youth laid out criteria that reflected youth issues and perspectives in the candidates' values, experience, and commitments—for example, a track record of "supporting student voice" and "putting words into action," and a commitment to "advocating for SAT supports for students." Youth also proposed and ran their own "fishbowl" hiring panel for the finalist candidates in which they used a rubric developed through consultation with the broader student and parent community to evaluate the candidates in key areas.

The student interview panel itself was highly diverse, with specific intention placed on including students from a range of geographic areas and grade levels (including middle and high school), and of various ethnicities, sexual orientations, and genders. After each interview, the board joined the youth in the room and youth reviewed their assessment of the candidates. When the new superintendent was announced in early May 2017, one of the first meetings she requested was with the youth panelists.

The Office of Student, Family, and Community Engagement has also worked to bring a culture of youth voice into the broader district community schools work. The OSFCE sits within the larger Community Schools and Student Services department, which houses behavioral health, restorative justice, after-school programming, health and wellness, among others. Each of these departmental units have a youth component within them.

The Health and Wellness unit has a Gay-Straight Alliance coordinator, who works with youth across the district to inform the LGBTQ rights curriculum. The After-school programming group works with after-school agencies across the city to develop youth leaders. The African American Male Achievement initiative has a student council. And the Restorative

Justice unit has intentionally created youth intern positions to advise and support (as well as receive training) the restorative justice work across the district.

Additionally, the Restorative Justice unit has funded a staff position dedicated to support youth engagement in restorative justice, leading to the development of hundreds of middle school and high school peer restorative justice leaders who take on the role of "culture keepers" on their campuses and lead restorative justice circles. Adult allies working in the OSFCE still perceive they have more work to do, but the district has come a long way. Additionally, the student activist goals of student supports, quality teaching, and positive culture/climate are still central to the district's vision of the community schools work (for the System Strategy Map articulating OUSD community school goals, strategies, and outcomes [see figure 7.3]).

Challenges and Opportunities

Making room for youth voice in community schools is about creating the climate and conditions that will permit youth to take on participatory roles on a widespread scale. While making room for youth voice in community schools certainly involves new competencies and skills for youth, it also involves new mindsets for adults, not to mention substantive shifts in school organizational culture and practices. All of this takes substantive effort, and cannot live with one person, one office, or one program alone.

This sentiment was echoed by OUSD staff. When asked to reflect on the progress of the student engagement work, staff stated that the biggest challenge and opportunity was working with adults. This includes work with adult allies, as well as adults in schools more generally. Adult allies—those who wholeheartedly believe in the potential of young people to contribute their strengths and skills for the benefit of themselves and their communities—are usually staff at a community school who are willing to take on the role of advocate, ally, and mentor with youth.

In OUSD, an adult ally is often the adult responsible for running the school's leadership program. More district staff time to cultivate adult allies could support meaningful student engagement across more sites. While many committed adult allies have stepped into roles as "leadership coordinators" supporting youth at their school sites, district staff believe there could be more adults supporting the work.

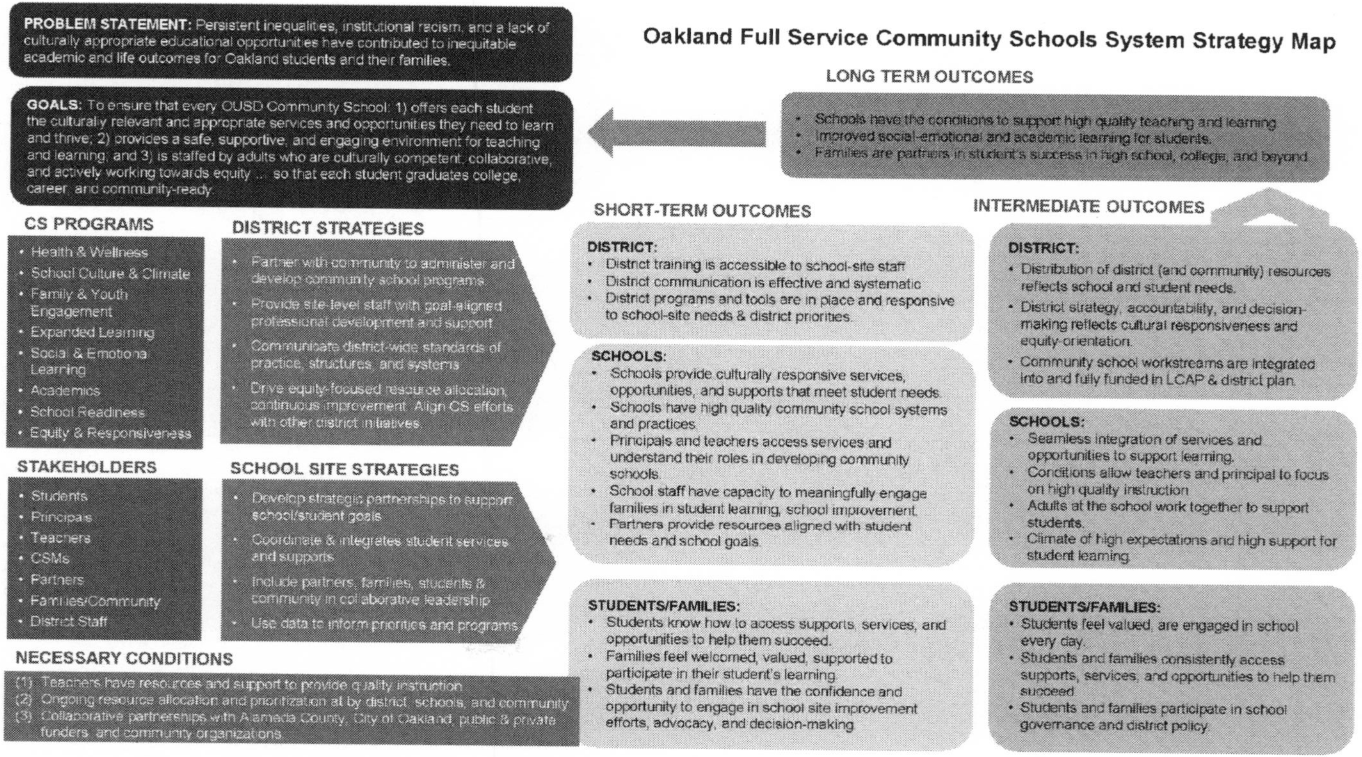

Oakland Full Service Community Schools System Strategy Map

PROBLEM STATEMENT: Persistent inequities, institutional racism, and a lack of culturally appropriate educational opportunities have contributed to inequitable academic and life outcomes for Oakland students and their families.

GOALS: To ensure that every OUSD Community School: 1) offers each student the culturally relevant and appropriate services and opportunities they need to learn and thrive; 2) provides a safe, supportive and engaging environment for teaching and learning; and 3) is staffed by adults who are culturally competent, collaborative, and actively working towards equity ... so that each student graduates college, career and community-ready.

LONG TERM OUTCOMES

- Schools have the conditions to support high quality teaching and learning
- Improved social-emotional and academic learning for students
- Families are partners in student's success in high school, college, and beyond

INTERMEDIATE OUTCOMES

DISTRICT:
- Distribution of district (and community) resources reflects school and student needs
- District strategy, accountability, and decision-making reflects cultural responsiveness and equity orientation
- Community school workstreams are integrated into and fully funded in LCAP & district plan

SCHOOLS:
- Seamless integration of services and opportunities to support learning
- Conditions allow teachers and principal to focus on high-quality instruction
- Adults at the school work together to support students
- Climate of high expectations and high support for student learning

STUDENTS/FAMILIES:
- Students feel valued, are engaged in school every day
- Students and families consistently access supports, services, and opportunities to help them succeed
- Students and families participate in school governance and district policy

SHORT-TERM OUTCOMES

DISTRICT:
- District training is accessible to school-site staff
- District communication is effective and systematic
- District programs and tools are in place and responsive to school-site needs & district priorities

SCHOOLS:
- Schools provide culturally responsive services, opportunities, and supports that meet student needs
- Schools have high quality community school systems and practices
- Principals and teachers access services and understand their roles in developing community schools
- School staff have capacity to meaningfully engage families in student learning, school improvement
- Partners provide resources aligned with student needs and school goals

STUDENTS/FAMILIES:
- Students know how to access supports, services, and opportunities to help them succeed
- Families feel welcomed, valued, supported to participate in their student's learning
- Students and families have the confidence and opportunity to engage in school site improvement efforts, advocacy, and decision-making

CS PROGRAMS
- Health & Wellness
- School Culture & Climate
- Family & Youth Engagement
- Expanded Learning
- Social & Emotional Learning
- Academics
- School Readiness
- Equity & Responsiveness

DISTRICT STRATEGIES
- Partner with community to administer and develop community school programs
- Provide site-level staff with goal-aligned professional development and support
- Communicate district-wide standards of practice, structures and systems
- Drive equity-focused resource allocation, continuous improvement. Align CS efforts with other district initiatives

SCHOOL SITE STRATEGIES
- Develop strategic partnerships to support school/student goals
- Coordinate & integrates student services and supports
- Include partners, families, students & community in collaborative leadership
- Use data to inform priorities and programs

STAKEHOLDERS
- Students
- Principals
- Teachers
- CSMs
- Partners
- Families/Community
- District Staff

NECESSARY CONDITIONS
(1) Teachers have resources and support to provide quality instruction
(2) Ongoing resource allocation and prioritization at by district, schools, and community
(3) Collaborative partnerships with Alameda County, City of Oakland, public & private funders and community organizations

Figure 7.3.   OUSD Community Schools and Student Services System Strategy Map 2017/18

Additionally, district staff would like to provide more training to a broader range of adults at the school site, not just leadership coordinators, to help adults at the school site learn the skills and competencies to partner with students. Otherwise, if young people are learning new skills and competencies but adults are not skilled at responding, it gives young people the message to "not have faith" in themselves, their school, and the potential to enact meaningful change. All of this work takes time and resources. While the OSFCE has an amazing team of dedicated staff, their time is finite, and the needs are great.

Making room for youth participation also requires adults to slow down and listen—something incredibly challenging in busy school contexts. In the words of one community school manager and adult ally:

> When our students show up, we give the thumbs up. We listen. You hit the breaks, we hit pause, we're going to listen. Yeah, we get busy. Yeah, adults can sometimes be focused on whatever. But when kids say, "this is going on, we need to fix it," we're on it. It's key that our kids can say, "time out, you're too much of an adult right now." We can take the pause, see what we're missing, ask them to explain it to us . . . Never forget that no one is more familiar with the experience than someone who's receiving it. You're never going to get better information about what's working for students than actually talking to them and letting them lead something. You're just not.

In community schools, which are built on the premise of being responsive to the needs of the community, students must be counted as part of that community.

In terms of where the work will go from here, the OSFCE is working on strengthening youth engagement in state-mandated school site governance—for example, the LCAP process described above, along with the Single Plan for Student Achievement (SPSA), a school improvement plan aligned to California Department of Education policy and the Every Student Succeeds Act. These traditionally adult-dominated structures present powerful opportunities for youth to have a voice in binding decisions on school priorities, spending decisions, and important outcomes. Meaningful youth participation in these spaces will require scaffolding and support (for youth and adults!), and presents an exciting next opportunity for the youth engagement work in Oakland.

FINAL THOUGHTS

Community schools can be a powerful strategy for expanding and enhancing student learning. Through offering integrated student supports, expanded learning opportunities, and parental engagement, community schools can bolster protective factors for youth and enhance student achievement. However, community schools also have the potential to do more. Serving the "whole child," making room for partner organizations in school leadership and decision making, promoting a collaborative, engaged school culture/climate, and making efforts to include the broader school community in meaningful ways are all hallmarks of community schools.

Community schools represent an expanded vision of what a school does to promote learning, who is included in its organizational mission and operation, and how it uses time and resources in order to increase educational equity. While families, youth, and partners are intentionally incorporated into community school organization and culture, community schools have the potential to expand that vision to include young people not only as recipients of education, but also as critical and engaged stakeholders.

OUSD has come a long way in creating the conditions for meaningful student engagement. Students were part of selecting the district's superintendent. They have influenced core district policy regarding graduation requirements, credit recovery, and school nutrition. The MSE standards have set a precedent for student and adult expectation around student participation in educational decision-making. While Oakland students and adult allies are likely to say there is still much to do in terms of growing a culture of young peoples' voices impacting practice, the experience of youth in OUSD's community schools reflects a powerful approach to making space for youth.

The story of youth voice in OUSD community schools requires understanding the rich tapestry of civic engagement and youth organizing that predates the community schools work. It also underscores how a focus on equity created common language between student activists and adult staff. It also shows how students can be powerful forces in engaging with data, leveraging community wisdom, building collaborative relationships across stakeholders, demanding shared accountability, and ultimately, catalyzing powerful school and district improvement.

One lesson youth and adult allies have been learning as they engage with more adults across school and district offices is that the things that students are frustrated about (e.g., low graduation rates, disproportionate suspensions for students of color, and poor credit recovery) are things that adults are frustrated about as well. Seeing that "we're on the same page" can propel continued meaningful partnership between youth leaders and adult staff.

Many of the district's key initiatives over the last decade, such as restorative justice practices, school-based health centers, and community schools, have been pushed for by students. Continuing to include students not only in the development of these policies, but also their implementation (e.g., hiring decisions, program evaluation) could be an enormous step in bringing in student voice at the system level, strengthening the whole child approach, and improving overall educational experiences and outcomes for youth.

As the ultimate "users" of public education, students offer important insight into how programs, policies, and instruction are actually being experienced in the classroom, in schools, and in the community. Yet, how many schools nationwide are engaging students in meaningful ways? How many districts?

If OUSD students are any indication, students want to know about program quality and access. They want to know how their schools are serving young people from different backgrounds. They want to make sure all students have access to safe schools, quality teachers, and the supports they need to succeed. These are goals that most adults in education—teachers, parents, school administrators, and district staff—also share. Ensuring that young people are part of the decisions impacting their educational experience and futures not only makes sense, it may be necessary for meaningful change.

REFERENCES

Alameda County Public Health Department (August 2008). Life and death from unnatural causes: Health and social inequity in Alameda County. http://www .acphd.org/media/53628/unnatcs2008.pdf.

Cervone, B., & Cushman, K. (2002). Moving youth participation into the classroom: Students as allies. In B. Kirshner, J. O'Donoghue, M. McLaughlin

(Eds.), *Youth participation: Improving institutions and communities* (pp. 83–99). New Directions for Youth Development, No. 96. San Francisco: Jossey-Bass.

Dryfoos, J. (2005). Full-service community schools: A strategy—not a program. In J. Dryfoos, & J. Quinn (Eds). *Community schools: A strategy for integrating youth development and school reform* (p. 7–14), New Directions for Youth Development, No. 107. San Francisco: Jossey-Bass.

Eccles, J., & Gootman, J. A. (Eds.). (2002). *Community programs to promote youth development*. Washington, D.C.: National Academies Press.

Fehrer, K., & Leos-Urbel, J. (2015). *Oakland unified school district community schools: Supporting students, teacher, and families*. Stanford, CA: John W. Gardner Center for Youth and Their Communities.

Fehrer, K., Leos-Urbel, J. (2016). "We're One Team": Examining community school implementation strategies in Oakland. *Educ. Sci. 6*, 26.

Ginwright, S., & James, T. (2002). From assets to agents of change: Social justice, organizing, and youth development. In B. Kirshner, J. O'Donoghue, & M. McLaughlin (Eds.), *Youth participation: Improving institutions and communities* (pp. 27–46). New Directions for Youth Development, No. 96. San Francisco: Jossey-Bass.

Goldwasser, M. (2004). *A guide to facilitate action research for youth*. Philadelphia, PA: Research for Action.

Kids First Oakland (2017). Victories and milestones. https://www.oaklandkidsfirst.org/about-us/wins/. Accessed 3/15/2018.

Kirshner, B. (2015). *Youth activism in an era of education inequality*. New York: NYU Press.

McLaughlin, M. (2000). "Community Counts: How Youth Organizations Matter for Youth Development." Washington, DC: Public Education Network.

Salusky, I., Larson, R., Griffith, A., Wu, J., Raffaelli, M., Sugimura, N., & Guzman, M. (2014). How adolescents develop responsibility: What can be learned from youth programs. In *Journal of Research on Adolescence, 24*(3). 417–430.

Shah, S., & Mediratta, K. (2008). Negotiating reform: Young people's leadership in the educational arena. In S. Deschenes, M. McLaughlin, & A. Newman (Eds.), *Community organizing and youth advocacy* (p. 43–59). New Directions for Youth Development, No. 117. San Francisco: Jossey-Bass.

Warren, M., Mira, M., & Nikundiwe, T. (2008). Youth organizing: From youth development to school reform. In S. Deschenes, M. McLaughlin, & A. Newman (Eds.), *Community organizing and youth advocacy* (p. 27–42). New Directions for Youth Development, No. 117. San Francisco: Jossey-Bass.

Chapter Eight

Community School Partnerships and Continuous Improvement

Adeline Ray and Carl Egner

The Chicago Public Schools (CPS) Community Schools Initiative (CSI) is part of a social justice movement taking place in cities, large and small, across the country. Mobilizing the resources and expertise of communities to remove barriers to learning and enrich and expand the breadth of each child's experiences is a clear statement of belief that education goes way beyond the closed system of a school comprised of teachers and students in classrooms. In community schools, education is a communal and collective endeavor that requires sustainable, intentional, and aligned results-focused partnerships.

All the players in the endeavor—community organizers, teachers, resource coordinators, families, students, school leaders, social service specialists, out-of-school time providers, district leaders, evaluators, funders, government agencies, and schools of higher education—are critical components working within the community schooling strategy to improve the lives of children.

The district-led CSI has a long history of developing and supporting community schools, and in recent years has created a comprehensive quality improvement process that is now being implemented across all CSI community schools together with their aligned partners. This chapter describes the role of community school partnerships, and how the use of a robust quality improvement process is helping to further community schooling in Chicago, and ultimately to gather the resources of the community around supporting the achievement and success of students and their families.

HOW DID WE GET HERE?

Chicago Public Schools administers one of the largest and longest running community schools programs in the country. It began in 1996 as an initiative of a local foundation, the Polk Bros. Foundation's "Full Service Schools Initiative" (FSSI). After an evaluation found positive outcomes, the district, led by then Chief Executive Officer Arne Duncan, scaled up the pilot strategy.

In 2002, through a public–private partnership with the philanthropic community, Duncan set a goal to open over 100 community schools within five years. Since then, the district's Community Schools Initiative has transformed more than 250 elementary and high schools into community schools. CPS is the nation's third-largest school district serving 371,000 students in 646 schools, as of this writing.

Community school partnerships have been key to transforming the way school sites operate. These partnerships bring together the academic and social supports needed to ensure that all students succeed by offering programs before, during, and after the school day for students and their families. The programs are designed to support the school's academic program and expand the services offered within the community.

Programs available at each community school vary based on the school's needs and local assets, but most community schools in Chicago offer some combination of academic enrichment activities for students, adult education, and English as a Second Language classes, student and adult technology training, art activities, recreation, and health services.

The community schools affiliated with the CSI share a number of core distinguishing features. CSI schools assert a strong link between addressing students' psychosocial well-being and effective support for student learning. In particular, the improvement of student learning is linked to the accomplishment of three operational objectives:

- To broaden and deepen the range of services, resources, and developmental opportunities available to students in ways that promote student well-being and attachment to school, address academic and psychosocial deficits, and promote positive development;
- To address the needs of parents and families, and strengthen the parent–school relationship as an asset to student learning; and

- To link classrooms and teachers to community resources and professionals in ways that support student learning.

These three key objectives are accomplished through the implementation at each school site of the CSI community school model that includes
the following core elements:

- Engaging at least one nonprofit lead partner agency (LPA) to collaborate with school administrators in connecting the school with other
  community resources, supporting planning activities, and providing
  some direct services;
- Hiring a full-time Community School Resource Coordinator (RC) with
  the primary responsibility for developing and managing student and
  adult programs in partnership with key school and agency staff;
- Developing a Community School Advisory Committee for planning
  and oversight of community school activities that broadly represents
  community stakeholders, especially those who do or can contribute to
  improved student learning and the further development of the community school (e.g., teachers, parents, social service providers, community-
  based organizations [CBOs], churches, and local business people);
- Deepening sources of information about the needs and desires of students, families, and other community school participants upon which to
  base the development of new strategies, resources, and programs; and
- Extension of the time in which the school building is open and in use,
  typically to include activities in the evening hours, with adequate security and physical plant support.

These elements are similar to other community schools around the
country (e.g., see the role of the coordinator in chapter 5). The elements
also align with the Coalition for Community Schools' National Community School Standards.[1]

We learned over time, however, that having all those components in
place was not sufficient to universally affect positive outcomes for students and their families. In 2005 we worked in partnership with our external evaluator at the University of Illinois at Chicago, Samuel P. Whalen,
PhD, to develop the CSI Logic Model in order to guide community school
planning and implementation.

Next, around 2009, with the logic model in hand, an internal CSI evaluation team comprised of doctoral candidates from the University of Illinois at Chicago set about defining the components in place at high-performing community schools. LPAs and their staff, as well as principals, teachers, parents, and students played a key role in this work. Taken from the playbooks of these important stakeholders, who shared their expertise in interviews, focus group discussions, and through field observations, the result is the *CSI Implementation and Sustainability Process Strategy, or ISPS* (see figure 8.1) (Zander, Burnside, & Poff, 2011).

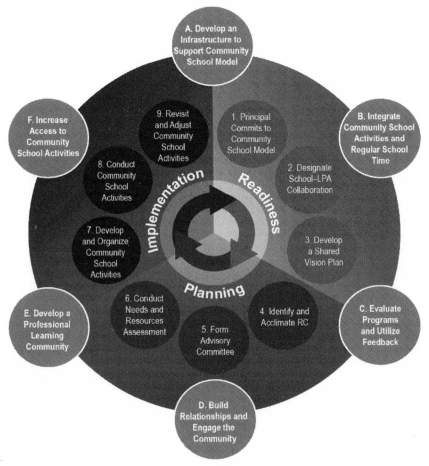

Figure 8.1.   CSI ISPS Graphic

The CSI ISPS is a standardized yet flexible strategy that created a common language among community school stakeholders to better evaluate and improve community schools throughout Chicago. The in-depth internal implementation evaluation and the resulting ISPS made a significant contribution to helping us understand how all Chicago community school partners, educators, and district administrators can more strategically realize positive student outcomes together.

Only through coordinated and deliberate effort can we have an impact that will transform the individual lives of children, and of schools and communities. In the following sections, we describe the essential role partners have in a community school, especially the lead partner, and how all partners and school staff utilize the ISPS for quality implementation and improvement.

LEAD PARTNER

In our experience, schools are simply not able on their own to meet all the needs of all students and their families who live in high-need communities (see ISPS Readiness step 2). To take just one example, many students in Chicago Public Schools come from families of recently arrived immigrants, and these students often have serious language, legal, and social-emotional needs. Partner agencies can provide a range of services and supports that, when organized strategically, allow students and families to thrive so that schools are able to fulfill their main educational mission.

The lead partner agency, or LPA, brings a new perspective to the school. By sharing the knowledge they have gained working with families, through the variety of services and programs they offer the community, they help teachers and school staff develop important insights and develop a deeper understanding of how to work more effectively with parents. Together with other members of the Community School Advisory Committee, they also help ensure that parents, teachers, students, and community members remain engaged in a common purpose.

The LPA hires and provides important guidance to the resource coordinator. In addition to leveraging the resources, programs, and services the LPA offer, the LPA also helps the resource coordinator identify and secure

services from a variety of sources to fill gaps in service and enhance offerings for students and adults. In addition, the LPA helps facilitate an active
and cooperative working relationship with the principal.

LPAs are identified by CPS through a pre-qualification process that
requires the submittal of an application and responses to interrogatories
that include descriptions on how the organization monitors the quality of
staff performance, how they will implement performance assurance guar-
antees based on the Chicago Board of Education's predetermined criteria,
and how the agency will engage the community to sustain the community
school strategy beyond the funding term.

Applications are scored by a review committee. Selected agencies
must then be formally approved by the Chicago Board of Education.
This process leads to a contract with the district that names partnership
implementation agreements, required programming, and key performance
measures including:

- Employing the CSI Continuous Quality Improvement Process at par-
  ticipating schools;
- Prioritizing off-track students and students in transitional living situa-
  tions for recruitment and participation;
- Including school staff, adult family, and community members, as well
  as other agencies in the CSI Advisory Committees;
- Schools will show improvement on a variety of measures on the *My Voice,
  My School Parent Survey* as reported by parents, and the 5Essentials
  Surveys as reported by students and teachers. Both surveys are built on
  the *5Essentials* developed by the University of Chicago Consortium on
  School Research at the University of Chicago Urban Education Institute,
  in partnership with Chicago Public Schools; and
- Students attending 120 hours or more of programming over two years
  show an improvement in core class grades and on-track rates, when
  compared to the previous year. And schools will show academic improvement on state assessment math/reading scores for students who
  attended 120 hours or more of programming over 2 years.

The approximately 30 LPAs approved through this process come from
a variety of different areas. These organizations include arts-based (Columbia College, Chicago), youth development (Youth Guidance), social

service (Metropolitan Family Services), higher education (Loyola University, Chicago), health (YMCA of Metro Chicago), and community-based (Enlace Chicago). In addition to bringing their unique programmatic and service focus to our community schools, a part of an LPA's strength is the ability to partner with additional organizations to balance services provided within the school building.

ADDITIONAL PARTNERS

LPAs are only the first partnership a CSI community school forms. The LPA serves as a managing partner, coordinating and collaborating with all the district and agency resources coming into the school building in order to avoid duplication of programming and services and to ensure all resources are used to their fullest extent.

An LPA, and their RC, work to bring in additional partnerships to fill any gaps, and in some cases, they say "no" to potential partnerships that do not meet the vision or mission of the community school. In order to stay focused on results and aligned with the school's mission, partnership for partnership's sake just won't suffice. An LPA must recognize and contribute the partner's expertise, then work with the community school leadership to bring in, or subcontract, those expert services that are needed at the community school.

As of this writing, over 150 different partners are engaged across the 65 district-managed community schools. These range greatly in size, area of expertise, role in relation to the school, and in many other areas as well. In addition to the LPA, partners bring many different types of experience and expertise to these schools. Some, like the Illinois Youth Soccer Association or the professional Chicago Fire Soccer Club, bring a high degree of expertise to after-school programs that are in high demand at many of our schools.

Other partners bring a different type of expertise to programs, like Common Threads, an organization that arranges for professional chefs to teach cooking and nutrition classes, or the First Tee that teaches basic golfing skills. Several of our schools work with local community colleges to provide ESL or GED programs. Other colleges and universities partner with our schools to provide tutors or program staff. One of the LPAs also has arranged for programming from the WE Day program—an international organization that encourages young people to become actively involved in issues in their community.

Partners can do more than provide programming. Some schools, for example, partner with local issue-advocacy groups that come to the school to provide information for parents and other community members. Local businesses can provide meeting space, food, or materials. Most importantly, the community school's partners must share a vision and align their efforts. Committing to continuous quality improvement efforts is essential to effective, high-quality partnerships.

QUALITY IMPROVEMENT

The CSI recognized early on that its initial logic model was not enough to assure quality or fidelity of implementation. The ISPS, an even more detailed logic model, was still not enough to guarantee fidelity to the community school model in practice, nor guarantee that the highest quality programs and services were being delivered. The need for something more became abundantly clear to CSI leadership when CPS first adopted the "school turnaround" strategy to *repair* failing schools in 2006.

School turnaround meant firing the entire staff, from the principal, to teachers, to classroom aides, to clerks, to security guards and maintenance staff, and replacing them with, in many cases, an entirely new team of adults. This was followed a few years later by wholesale school closures, leaving many communities without their singular community anchor, their neighborhood public school. Finding CSI community schools on school turnaround or closure lists was discouraging, disheartening, and disappointing. It was also all too common since community schools tend to be those in the highest need communities.

Diving deeper into the ISPS to draw out the key elements that undergird what makes a community school highly functioning, the CSI joined with the American Institutes for Research and the Diehl Consulting Group to develop the Continuous Quality Improvement Process (CQIP). The CSI CQIP involves assessment of two key elements of community school implementation: the organizational (or school) level, and the point of service (activity) level.

The first element of the CQIP for assessing the organizational-level implementation is the Self-Assessment Quality Improvement Rubric. The rubric is divided into four domains:

1. Establish and maintain essential structures and resources needed for an effective community school.
2. Establish and maintain community school programs and services.
3. Establish and maintain continuous improvement structures.
4. Develop strategies and commit resources to financially and organizationally sustain the community school.

Each domain is divided into elements and sub-elements. The site-level community school team, usually in the form of its Community School Advisory Committee, assesses its stage of development for each sub-element: planning, emerging, proficient, or exemplary. In order to support schools with the CQIP, the district hired two CSI quality coaches who worked with the schools to develop their Advisory Committee and to get started with the scoring of the rubric.

Self-Assessment Quality Improvement Rubric in Practice

Admittedly, implementation and use of the CQIP has varied. Some community schools and their partners are immediately enthusiastic and dive right into using the tool. Others are much more resistant, and need a lot of encouragement to use it at all. The following example shows how schools and their partners have used the CQIP Youth Program Quality Assessment (YPQA) portion of the tool to make concrete improvements.

Sumner Elementary School is located on Chicago's West Side, a neighborhood that—even by Chicago standards—faces many economic and social challenges. The school population is over 98 percent African American, and about 95 percent low-income. The school is a welcoming oasis within the community, and they have developed a strong and effective Community School Advisory Committee.

The committee consists of several individuals with different kinds of connections to the school: school staff, students, parents, a local pastor, and various partners such as representatives from the local 4-H Club, from a foundation, and from a Chicago-based educational advocacy group. The Advisory Committee meets once a month for a working meeting where the members discuss concrete ways in which they are helping to raise the standard of their community school.

For example, after having scored the CQIP rubric together, the group decided that they needed a more robust process for using the YPQA program observation tool. The tool had been used by only two people but the Advisory Committee felt that having only two observers was too limited and also that only two people could not spend enough time in each class to make an informed evaluation.

This issue was brought to the whole committee and all the members were asked if they would be willing to participate. They agreed, so the committee spent an entire meeting training on the use of the YPQA tool. Then each member gave a day/time they were available to come in and observe programs. After committee members had done their observations, they met to process the results and to discuss if there were any trends that would indicate actions that needed to be taken.

Also, in discussing the CQIP rubric results, the committee realized that they probably were not doing enough to get feedback from all parties (students, parents, and teachers). Therefore, they created a short survey to be filled out in each class for students and teachers. They use the results of the surveys to inform decisions about programming. They also created a parent survey for parents to complete on report card pick-up day.

YPQA in Practice

For the point-of-service part of the CQIP, the Youth Program Quality Assessment (YPQA) short form is employed. This validated tool, developed by the Weikart Center for Youth Program Quality, is designed to be used by trained observers. The YPQA assesses the following dimensions of community school programs:

1. Physical and Psychological Safety;
2. Appropriate Structure;
3. Supportive Relationships;
4. Opportunities to Belong;
5. Positive Social Norms;

6. Support for Efficacy and Mattering;
7. Opportunities for Skill Building;
8. Integration of Families, Schools, and Communities; and
9. Continuous Improvement.

The YPQA, the second main component of the CSI CQIP, is used by the CSI program coordinators as a key part of their work supporting CPS community schools centrally.

Some of the lead partner agencies—for example Metropolitan Family Services (MFS) and the YMCA of Metropolitan Chicago—have also incorporated the YPQA into their work. MFS program supervisors, for example, and school-site resource coordinators are all trained to use the YPQA. The MFS program supervisors go to different schools within MFS's network, observe programs, and report on their findings. This occurs ideally two to three times each school year. The observers then provide feedback to the schools through completing the YPQA score sheet (MFS uses the YPQA long form, whereas CSI uses the YPQA short form) and writing up a detailed report about the observation.

The YPQA Short Form done by CSI and the YPQA Long Form done by partners such as MFS run in parallel. Conducting different program observations at different times is useful because more programs are observed, though a need exists to develop ways to better coordinate the observations and the feedback for programmatic improvements. The following example of a site visit shows how this can work.

> At one of our CSI schools we arranged for the YPQA spring observation to be focused on two programs that the school had recently instituted. These were mentoring programs for middle school-aged students, one for girls and one for boys. The school specifically requested that we observe these two programs, because they were new and the school felt that they both were still finding their way.
>
> In addition, we arranged for the programs to be observed on the same day by the CSI Program Coordinator and the Program Supervisor from the LPA (which in this case was MFS).
>
> On the day of the observation, the two observers sat together off to the side of the room where the programs were taking place. Both programs, the one for the girls and the one for the boys, took place in the same room, the school's "multi-purpose" room that serves as both a cafeteria and a

gymnasium. The room is large and the two groups of students were both seated at tables in the same area of the room, close enough that they could hear each other.

Both groups had about 15 students and one adult program leader. Both programs used long tables that made it difficult for students sitting at one end of the table to hear the students at the other end. It also seemed apparent to the observers that both program leaders were having some trouble engaging the students. They would often ask questions but the students would not respond. On the other hand the students were sometimes talking among each other in side conversations that were not related to what the program leaders were trying to accomplish.

It was quickly obvious to both observers that this program had some serious issues that needed to be addressed. In fact, we did not even stay to the end of the program, but left before the end of the session to discuss what would be the best way to provide feedback.

The two observers decided that each would write up a separate formal report, as usual, but that there would be only one formal communication to the school about the observation. They decided that this communication would come from the CSI Program Coordinator, however both observers decided together on the content of this communication. They decided to point out some of the difficulties with the program, but also to make some concrete recommendations about how it could be improved. These included finding a better room where the two groups could each have some privacy, seating the students in a circle rather than at long tables, and finding a curriculum that would be more engaging for the students.

We sent this communication to the school. The principal quickly reacted by writing that the two programs should each move to their own classroom. The RC also committed to researching and finding a curriculum for the programs that would be more adapted to the needs of the students. The school purchased a new curriculum a few weeks later.

For the program observation the following fall, the school again asked that we observe the same programs. This time, however, the CSI Program Coordinator did the observation alone and was only able to observe the girls' program.

The difference from the previous observation was striking and immediately apparent. The program was situated in a small classroom, that gave the group total privacy with the girls seated in a circle. The use of the new curriculum also seemed to have helped. The group entered right away into a conversation that apparently was a continuation of the previous session. The atmosphere in the group was warm and congenial. The girls seemed to know each other well, to be happy to be there, and to be on positive terms with the program leader.

This example demonstrates how partners and schools may utilize a continuous improvement tool to strengthen students' experiences.

FINAL THOUGHTS

The Chicago community school model is built around the idea of partnerships. Dr. Patricia Harvey, a former chief accountability officer at CPS, once stated that community schools are, "A strategy for organizing the resources of the community around student success." High quality, results-focused, and aligned partnerships are crucial in order to successfully organize resources and transform the way our schools operate.

The partners described in this chapter are great examples of the kinds of partnerships we have built over time in Chicago. Many have developed strong systems to train and support their staff based in community schools. They have developed long-term partnerships with some schools to the point that these schools consider the support that partners bring to their students and communities as totally integral to their mission as a school.

At the same time, all partners have their own institutional strengths. There are social service agencies, youth development agencies, and other community-based organizations that have cultivated a real expertise in serving the students and families of their community schools. There are other areas of need that fall a bit more outside the area of the partner's particular area of expertise.

For example, the YMCA of Metro Chicago is one of our strong lead partners, and they provide a variety of programming for students. At some of their schools, however, the parents asked for GED or ESL programs for adults. In order to provide this, the YMCA contacted some local community colleges who were able to provide these services.

At CSI we are fond of saying that community schools are *more* than just a set of good after-school programs. But what is the "more" that we are talking about? For our community schools and partner agencies the "more" includes the core parts of Chicago's community school strategy, such as developing a voice for parents in decision making, or doing outreach in the school communities. These practices add value to school–community partnerships and are brought to light by the use of the self-assessment rubric that is so essential to creating meaningful partnerships.

This is why the CSI CQIP as a whole is an invaluable tool for our work in community schooling. Because it covers *all* the necessary ingredients in building a high-functioning community school, it allows schools and partners to recognize and affirm the areas where they are already strong, but also to identify and clarify areas that need improvement. Schools and their partners are continuously learning, together.

Furthermore, the CSI CQIP helps to smooth out challenges that inevitably occur in any partnership strategy. One of the biggest challenges we face, for example, is a change in key personnel. When a dedicated principal or an outstanding RC leaves a community school, it can almost force the school to start over from scratch as a community school.

Having the CSI CQIP as a record of what has happened previously, of the goals and action plans, can help a school, its partners, and families and community members to know where to focus their energies even after a major change occurs, and to ensure that change is intentional, comprehensive, and sustainable. Community schools working with partners become hubs of their neighborhoods, and this radiates out to transform the culture of the school, community, and district.

We have seen successful outcomes in those CSI school partnerships where the CQIP is used with a high degree of fidelity, schools we refer to as "higher implementing" community school. School-day absences for youth in grades nine to twelve at high implementing schools demonstrate significantly fewer absences than youth enrolled in lower implementing schools (Naftzger, Williams, & Liu, 2014). The effect is even greater when compared to youth in similar non-CSI schools.

Here we have learned that students in grades 9–12 have 61 percent fewer school-day absences. Student participation in higher implementing CSI schools is also associated with higher scores on the 5Essentials Survey on scales such as Academic Personalism, Psychological Sense of Membership, and Student-Teacher Trust. When compared to non-CSI counterparts, students in grades 9–12 were found to have more positive educational experiences; students in grades 4–8 had higher Emotional Health scores on the survey; and students in grades K–3 had significantly fewer suspensions and misconducts (Naftzger, et al, 2014). These results support our conclusion that Chicago's schools are stronger because of the partnerships that have mobilized to support them.

REFERENCES

Naftzger, N., Williams, R., & Liu, F. (2014). *Chicago Public Schools Community Schools Initiative evaluation: 2011–12 impact report.*

Zander, K., Burnside, E., & Poff, M. (2011). *The development of an Implementation and Sustainability Process Strategy (ISPS) for the Chicago Public Schools Community Schools Initiative: Findings and recommendations.*

Chapter Nine

The Role of the School District

Alison McArthur, Kelly Noser, and Tony Majors

School districts across the country are exploring ways to address the non-academic factors that impact their students, while maintaining a focus on improving instructional practices and student academic performance outcomes. Public education in America involves an ever-evolving and, at times, contentious debate about what programs, policies, and practices are most effective. However, most can agree that providing a quality education to children is a top priority.

In order for youth to take full advantage of the opportunities provided to them in school, we must address the increasingly difficult social, emotional, and environmental barriers they face. Educators and policy makers are increasingly spending more time and resources exploring how trauma, adverse childhood experiences, poverty, and socio-emotional supportive instructional programs impact school and student capacity to teach and learn.

Community schools are a place where schools, partners, parents, and community come together to address the barriers to learning that are unique to each school's community, while at the same time providing excellent learning experiences. School districts benefit from implementing a strategy that aligns school and community resources strategically and equitably. Partners and school leaders select interventions that are individualized to child and school needs. Community schools answer the need to support the whole child and, ultimately, the whole community.

In this chapter, we outline some of the ways that the Metropolitan Nashville Public School System (MNPS) is addressing these issues through the alignment of internal and external resources, combined with building district and school capacity to implement and sustain the community school strategy, thereby expanding supports and improving outcomes for students. We offer these stories and practices as lessons learned for other districts creating a community school strategy and for partners working with districts.

MNPS used momentum and lessons learned from development of a single community school site in order to develop a district-led system of community schools. Our district has maintained a focus on purposeful expansion and implementation with fidelity by developing a results-based framework to guide schools in their unique site-based development while maintaining the tenets of the framework.

THE EVOLUTION OF A DISTRICTWIDE FOCUS ON COMMUNITY SCHOOLS: ONE DISTRICT'S JOURNEY

The focus on community schools in Nashville has evolved over the past decade as the district, Nashville community organizations, and one school community (Glencliff High School) explored the strategy. In 2009, MNPS formed a transformation team of district administrators and representatives from community organizations to explore the potential for the development and implementation of a system-wide community school strategy to address the complex whole student, school, and community needs.

School officials and community members recognized that there were large numbers of disenfranchised youth not attending or not successful in school. The students faced barriers around health, socio-economic status, and violence. With funding from a federal Substance Abuse and Mental Health Services Administration (SAMHSA) Mental Health Integration grant, MNPS sent a team of school-level representatives to the 2010 Coalition for Community Schools National Forum to learn more about how the community school strategy could improve district schools.

In addition to community participation in the district's transformation team, a Nashville-based community partner, Alignment Nashville, hosted a presentation by the Children's Aid Society on the community school strategy and research. Simultaneously, the transformation of Nashville's Glencliff High School into a community school contributed significantly to today's initiative.

In the 2009–2010 school year, Glencliff was not unlike many urban high schools facing high-stakes accountability. With an on-time graduation rate of 61 percent and other indicators of low academic performance, the state identified Glencliff as a "priority school," requiring it to transition to a new administration. Glencliff represented an extremely diverse population with a high percentage of English language learners. Due to high incidents of violence and gang activity, the district and school community were concerned about the safety of the school.

Through a U.S. Department of Education Small Learning Communities grant awarded in 2006, Glencliff had already reformed its instructional program using Career Academies.[1] While this was a powerful and significant reform effort, it did not address many factors impacting conditions for learning in the school. To address low academic performance, Glencliff needed to improve the school's climate and culture.

Administrators recognized a high rate of teen pregnancy among the students that led to increased rates of truancy and dropout as one contributing factor to poor performance, climate, and culture. To address the needs of the pregnant and parenting students, Glencliff administrators called on a group of community leaders, nonprofit representatives, and university partners for help. These partners created the Glencliff Community Coalition (GCC), signifying the initial development of a network of results-focused partnerships and the beginning of a full-service community school strategy.

Partners mobilized to address the challenges Glencliff students were facing. The GCC included partnerships with public and university-based childcare centers willing to enroll children of Glencliff students on an income-based sliding-scale. Other key partnering organizations focused on health and wellness outcomes.

The school developed a reputation as a resource to young parents and fewer pregnant and parenting students fell through the cracks. Meeting the academic and non-academic needs of the students and community became a core component to the school's reform efforts. Glencliff continued to reform its instructional model through Career Academies and sought other opportunities and partnerships to address non-academic student needs, adding meaningful value and opportunities for its students and parents. Stakeholders' perception of the school changed significantly as more students, teachers, parents, and community members saw the merit in strategic partnerships.

By the spring of 2011, the school had developed partnerships that provided direct academic supports (e.g., exploratory learning opportunities, dual enrollment, industry certifications, online credit recovery programs, and an expanded leadership model) and services to support the conditions for learning (e.g., physical and mental health services, mentoring programs, language and mentoring programs for English language learners and families, and positive youth development programs).

The partnerships and programs, combined with high expectations for instruction, behavior, and student academic performance resulted in substantial improvements in both culture and academic performance. Glencliff, once a school targeted for improvement, met or exceeded state academic performance benchmarks and transitioned to "in good standing" status. The Coalition for Community Schools awarded Glencliff the National Community School of Excellence Award.

Following this success, MNPS transitioned the executive principal, Tony Majors, to a district-level position as the assistant superintendent of support services, where he led the development of the district vision of how a school-based model could transform to a district-wide strategy for community schools. Community Achieves (CA), the MNPS community school initiative, was born.

Organize the Initiative around a Results-Based Framework

As MNPS integrated the community school strategy with its overall vision, they developed a CA Oversight Committee, representing community leaders from business, nonprofit, government, and education sectors. The committee provided important voice and expertise in the development of the CA strategy. Focusing on impact, the district deemed it important to have the voices of such a wide range of community stakeholders in decisions about the key results around which they were building the community school strategy. The Oversight Committee discussed issues facing the Nashville community and reviewed data on areas of need and gaps in support.

Based on their use of data and discussions, the committee proposed that CA focus on achieving results in four priority areas, becoming the "pillars of CA": Health and Wellness, Parent/Family Engagement, College and Career Readiness, and Social Services.

The four pillars give schools and partners concrete focus areas around which they can develop strategies, supported by needs assessments and root-cause analyses, best-practices, student- and school-level monitoring,

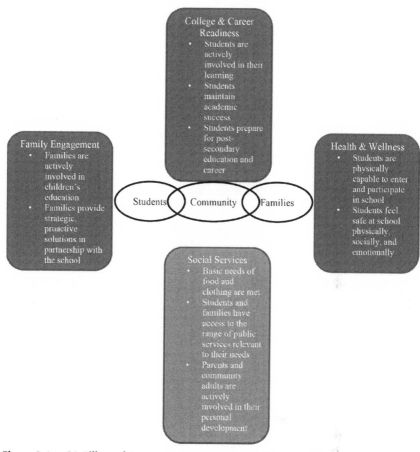

Figure 9.1. CA Pillars of Support

and continuous improvement. The committee also worked to identify corresponding outcomes within each pillar, based largely on data-availability (figure 9.1 presents outcome statements for each pillar).

Furthermore, the outcome statements have corresponding indicators that inform strategic planning. For example, indicators of family engagement outcomes include attendance at family events and participation in parent-teacher conferences; college and career readiness outcome indicators include chronic absence rates, scholarship dollars awarded, and standardized testing results; indicators of health and wellness outcomes include discipline incidents and school climate ratings; and social service outcome indicators include food distributions and numbers of adults in English language classes.

Develop a Unique, Scalable, Sustainable Framework

MNPS used Race to the Top funds, available from the U.S. Department of Education's largest ever competitive investment to reward reform efforts, to create a Community Achieves Office within the MNPS Department of Support Services. The office initially included a district-level coordinator, an administrative assistant, and a contracted evaluator, and later added a program specialist. The staff began a cycle of development and continuous improvement of the CA Framework, to guide a scalable and sustainable community schools framework.

CA staff utilized resources and networking opportunities provided by the Coalition for Community Schools in developing the strategy. CA created a peer-learning partnership with Oakland Unified School District, because of the similarities across the two districts in community school work, use of the academies model, and district partnerships with the Collaborative for Academic, Social, and Emotional Learning (CASEL), a national nonprofit, to embed social-emotional learning strategies.

The CA Framework, finalized in 2015, provides standards for school-site implementation. The CA office and community partners adapted the standards and best-practices of other national models to fit within the local context of the district, providing a structure to coordinate existing district departments and supports, as shown in figure 9.2. The four standards include school-level coordination, integration of community schools in the School Improvement Process, extended learning opportunities, and results-focused partnerships.

The framework included a corresponding rubric to guide school-level development. The CA roll-out strategy incorporated school selection, structures, processes, infrastructure, and technical assistance on the standards of the framework and tools to capture and utilize data related to the outcomes and indicators developed by the Oversight Committee. During the 2016–2017 school year, MNPS had 18 CA schools located in 9 of 12 geographic clusters throughout the district, including 5 elementary, 11 middle, and 2 high schools.

Expansion plans were to have approximately 32 schools with at least two schools in each geographic cluster serving a feeder pattern. Implementation levels of the framework varied across schools and years due to turnover in school or partner leadership, the coordinator role, and

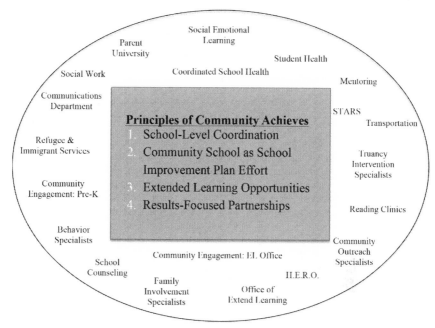

Figure 9.2. Using Community Achieves to Implement Full Service Community Schools

implementation strategies. A system of continuous improvement and self-assessment efforts helped to identify areas of strength and plans to address weaknesses recognized at both the school- and initiative-level.

BUILD INTERNAL CAPACITY
AT THE DISTRICT-LEVEL

While CA is a district-led initiative, it was crucial to educate other departments within the district on how the initiative can support their goals and objectives, and to create a shared understanding that mutual success relies on continuous interdepartmental collaboration and communication. To prevent siloed and duplicated efforts, other departments needed to know that the CA initiative is a framework, not a program, that will come into a school to make sweeping changes or take credit for improvements. Rather, it is an effort to individualize, align, and build supports based on a school community's needs, existing resources, and strategic improvement plans.

Align District Departmental Supports

The district's decision to take the lead as the intermediary in the community school strategy was based on an existing infrastructure of student supports and a school- and district-level track record of engaging the community. MNPS serves the entire geographic area of Davidson County, with a total of 88,761 students, divided into 12 geographic "clusters." MNPS provides *all* students in *all* schools with academic and non-academic support services.

MNPS organizes many support services staff in cluster support teams, serving each geographic cluster, which may have up to nine schools. Teams consist of Social Workers, Truancy Intervention Specialists, Family Involvement Specialists, Behavior Analysts, and a departmental Data Specialist. Other support services divisions that serve all schools include Student Health, Coordinated School Health, Extended Learning, Discipline, Homeless Education, Safe and Drug Free Schools, School-Based Mental Health, Restorative Practices, Social and Emotional Learning, Parent University, and Family Engagement University. Aligning all these district supports required intentionality and coordination. The CA office was well positioned to facilitate alignment around the vision and effort of the CA initiative.

The CA office also worked with other district departments outside of support services including Transportation, Nutrition Services, Curriculum and Instruction, Federal Programs, and Information Management and Decision Support. The CA office has taken primary responsibility to communicate the vision of CA to MNPS departments and identify tangible ways the strategy will support their initiatives and increase the impact of their school-based efforts.

For example, many MNPS schools offer reading clinics through the Curriculum and Instruction department to provide intensive, individualized one-on-one tutoring. At CA schools, CA site managers are available to develop partnerships to provide tutors from the community organizations that have access to individual volunteers willing to be trained and commit to tutoring with reading clinics throughout the school year. The CA site managers coordinate the volunteer efforts and engage organizations as results-focused partners.

Enhance School Capacity
for Implementation

In focusing on enhanced support for schools, the CA office works mainly with the 18 MNPS schools developing within the CA Framework. Some of these 18 schools were invited by district leadership based on priority status due to academic performance, or a geographic feeder pattern. Others self-selected to utilize the CA Framework because of a recognition of the overwhelming barriers to learning that students faced, stemming generally from adverse childhood experiences and poverty, which school administration believed a community school model could address.

The CA effort in all of these schools is coordinated by a school-level full-time CA site manager. This person, referenced above and also known in other initiatives as a community school coordinator (see chapter 4), works to increase the school's capacity to utilize the many supports provided by the district and those from external organizations that are organized around school needs as authentic results-focused partners.

The CA office has developed an annual cycle of school-level activities to facilitate implementation of the CA Framework. These include a developmental self-assessment of progress within the framework, a pillar-level needs assessment based on review of data on outcomes and resources within the four CA pillars (Health and Wellness, Parent/Family Engagement, College and Career Readiness, and Social Services), and strategic planning that aligns with the state-required School Improvement Plan.

Turnover and onboarding of school administrators and CA site managers means that individuals in those roles are always at different levels of understanding and implementation of the community school strategy. The CA office offers multiple differentiated trainings designed to address a variety of topics and levels of experience. Training includes data collection and analysis, district policies, meeting facilitation, and poverty simulation. The CA office provides infrastructure for monthly professional development topics for CA site managers, and technical assistance to capture, collect, manage, analyze, report, and utilize data on shared measures.

The CA office is intentional in building capacity of site managers and principals so that they can communicate a shared message and provide training to school and partner staff as necessary. CA site managers have transformed into a strong and supportive professional learning community. They attend training with the entire support services department throughout the year. Twice a year, school administrators receive training and updates on program monitoring, data collection, and best practices from schools excelling with implementation.

The CA office makes periodic school visits, with at least one annual visit that focuses on a semi-structured process of monitoring and facilitating implementation of the CA Framework, driven by schools' self-assessment and plans for addressing identified areas for improvement. Additionally, CA office staff work with site managers to facilitate convening of partners in school-level meetings that focus on shared data, review of programming cohorts of students, and development of a shared understanding of school needs, resources, and remaining gaps, in alignment with school improvement goals.

Use the District Office to Address District-Wide Needs and Solutions

With support from the CA office, schools and CA site managers build their capacity to identify programs and services that meet the needs of that school and community. However, there are issues and needs that span multiple schools or the entire district, which the CA office can more effectively address by serving as the intermediary. Some of the common needs include food, clothing, mentoring, and training on restorative practices. Additionally, some district and external partners have the capacity to put programming or supports in multiple schools. Working with the CA Office gives such partners the perfect platform to implement in multiple sites, potentially reaching more students and achieving greater impact.

For example, Nashville has food pantries across the city that distribute food regularly and in response to urgent situations, such as inclement weather. CA schools have established relationships with organizations that provide food donations and school-level CA staff to coordinate distribution logistics. This allows non-CA schools and their communities within the same geographic area to receive services otherwise unavailable.

Another example involves the widespread need for mentoring services across the district in CA and non-CA schools. Because of successful relationships built with organizations that provide mentoring in CA schools, the district has been able to use those partnerships as a resource to serve more students in non-CA schools.

BUILD EXTERNAL CAPACITY IN THE COMMUNITY

The environment in which any community school initiative develops is complex and dynamic. The capacity of city, district, and school communities to support and build successful community schools has wide variation and is ever-changing. Whether a community is rich with infrastructure partners that coordinate aspects of the initiative, like convening, recruiting, or aligning partners, or has a dearth of programming partners, development of a shared vision focused on results, collaboration, and alignment is a necessary component of supportive partnerships.

Just as school-level partners align supports with the needs of the school community, a district-led community school initiative must garner a broader base of support that aligns with the district's vision.

Collaborate with Community Leaders

In opting to develop a community school strategy led by the district, leaders of the CA initiative recognized early the importance of collaborating with key community leaders to guide the community school initiative's vision and strategy, build public will, and potentially, mobilize funding for developmental and sustainability purposes.

Collaborative work with Nashville's leaders began by identifying major organizations, departments, and offices across all sectors, including community organizers and leaders, nonprofit providers, universities and colleges, social service agencies, and government officials. Once the district identified the sector stakeholders, the CA office facilitated introductory meetings, school tours, information collection and data sharing on city needs. Many of these leaders became members of the Oversight Committee, as listed in table 9.1.

Table 9.1.

Community Achieves Oversight Committee	
ORGANIZATION	ROLE
Vanderbilt University	Dean Of Education And Human Development
Metro Nashville Juvenile Court	Metro Nashville Juvenile Judge
MNPS	Executive Director of Innovation
United Way	CEO
Ingram Industries	Vice President of Community Relations
Martha O'Bryan	President and CEO
Nashville Career Advancement Center	Director
Alignment Nashville and College and Career Readiness Liaison	Associate Executive Director
YMCA	CEO
MNPS	Associate Superintendent
Mayor's Office - NAZA	Director
MNPS	Community Achieves Coordinator
United Way and Social Services Liaison	Senior Director, Community Impact
Noser Consulting, LLC	External Evaluator
Metro Health Department	Director
Metro Social Services	Executive Director
MNPS Health and Wellness Liaison	Director Student Health
MNPS	Director Family Involvement and Community Services
Alignment Nashville	Executive Director
Chamber of Commerce	President and CEO
Conexión Américas	Executive Director
MNPS	Senior Secretary
MNPS	Magnet and Marketing Coordinator
PENCIL Foundation	Executive Director
MNPS	Assistant Director of Strategic Planning

As the district made progress through the initiative's developmental stages and was ready to move toward implementation in the schools, the Oversight Committee took on additional roles as advocates, an implementation monitoring body, and eventually assisted with branding of the initiative. In the beginning, this group met monthly for updates on progress and advice on emerging issues, reducing frequency bi-annually over a three-year period. As the CA initiative evolved, the large group split into two smaller groups; one focused on advocacy and action, the other focused on operations of programs and services.

Align External Resources with a Shared Vision

In addition to the many Nashville organizations that provide direct services to support students, families, and the community, there are multiple nonprofits in Nashville that support schools by aligning organizations, businesses, and resources to the district goals and school-level needs as part of a collective effort. Creating a system of CA schools allowed a unique opportunity to take collaboration to new heights, by identifying district- and school-level roles designed specifically to use community engagement to align resources at the district- and school-level.

The MNPS community school strategy incorporates collective impact as a defining feature, in that it represents the basis by which networks of support work together. Collective impact is a term to characterize systematic collaborative efforts from multiple people and organizations to move from a fragmented approach by many to a collective approach that is more than the sum of its parts (Kania & Kramer, 2011). CA defines the different types of partners that work collectively in alignment with school and district vision as follows:

- Anchor Partners operate at the district- and school-level, assist in strategic planning around the four pillars, advocate for the community school initiative, and create public will and policy. Most members of the Oversight Committee are Anchor Partners.
- Operational Partners provide school-level programming or services in support of the School Improvement Plan, often participate in the strategic planning process at the school-level, participate in the alignment of resources, and focus on a shared vision for the school.
- Co-located Partners provide programming or services at the schools to students, families, or community members with physical space in the school building or campus, but are not necessarily aware of their role within a collective approach.
- Supporting Partners volunteer time or make financial contributions and are not involved in strategic planning; these often include individual donors and faith-based organizations.

The CA office and school-level site managers are responsible for managing relationships with these different types of partners and providing the support they need to function within their roles, such as data sharing and details of School Improvement Plans.

Alignment of efforts across organizations that may compete with one another for funding and clients into a collective effort is a complex and often difficult task. However, we have found that increasing access to data and organizing partners around shared needs and outcomes with common measurement leads to better interaction and alignment. Placing the organizations' individual resources within a big picture approach to achieve the shared outcomes positions each of them as part of an overall solution, honoring their unique approaches.

Collaboration and alignment around a shared vision are imperative if communities are going to see change. Successful achievement of individual, organization, school, and system outcomes is more widespread and sustainable when school and partnering organizations' efforts are mutually supporting, and needs are addressed in a collective way.

BUILD INTERNAL CAPACITY AT THE SCHOOL-LEVEL AROUND STANDARDS

Even with the most comprehensive, coordinated, supported, and well-funded community school initiative, it's how that translates to meaningful change at the school-level that matters most. School-level coordination, integration and alignment with the school improvement plan, and community engagement are at the heart of a successful community school.

Develop School-Level Coordination

The CA Framework guides the training and capacity-building efforts that lead to full implementation of CA schools. The first standard of the framework focuses on school-level coordination. In the beginning years of developing Nashville's community school strategy, the first CA schools designated school-level positions to serve as the coordinators, as funding for a full-time Community School Manager had yet to be identified. Assistant principals, counselors, family involvement specialists, and others served in this coordination role.

After three years of implementation, the district opted to fund coordinators through the local operating budget, using the term CA Site Managers for this full-time position. As mentioned earlier, CA site managers are responsible for creating a connection with faculty, staff, principals, students, parents, MNPS departments, and community organizations. They also coordinate volunteers, acquire, schedule, and recruit programs/services, and in some cases, provide direct case management and referrals. The CA site managers coordinate programs and services provided by the school, the district, and external partners that support results within the four pillars of CA.

Schools also have formalized CA teams led by the CA site managers and school administration and made up of various stakeholders, which may include school counselors, social workers, school improvement team leaders, Title I facilitators, family engagement specialists, key community partners, parents, and students, among others. The CA team provides oversight, operational roles for community engagement, and multi-stakeholder perspectives. The teams have formal periodic agenda-driven meetings that focus on development, implementation, and sustainability within a continuous improvement approach aligned with the School Improvement Plan.

Align the Community School Approach with School Improvement Plan

Schools also monitor disaggregated and school-level data for specific programs (e.g., mentoring and tutoring) in order to identify areas of success and to determine mid-course corrections to programming, programming enrollment that is targeted and equitable, to recruit additional partners to support programming, and to ensure efforts are achieving results that the program is targeting (e.g., decreasing chronic absenteeism or discipline numbers).

The CA Framework provides guidance on how to align partners and programs with school and district goals identified in the School Improvement Plan. The work of the school and CA partners should not be separate, they must be in alignment as a comprehensive whole-school strategy. To support this alignment, CA teams engage in an annual needs assessment and strategic planning process.

This process involves teams assessing where they are in the CA implementation process using a rubric with a rating scale of emerging, maturing, or excelling. The school teams create strategic plans to communicate data and anecdotes, needs, existing efforts to meet those needs, and specific details of how partners can address these needs to support the school's needs as part of a results-focused partnership. Ideally, CA site managers and their teams update strategic plans continually, as the school communities monitor student data, implementation data, and remaining gaps between outcomes and efforts.

School-identified areas of focus, as communicated in School Improvement Plans, align to the district's vision and initiatives, and drive community supports offered to students, families, and the school community. To coordinate supports for students, families, and the community around these areas of focus, site managers continually take stock of existing resources and supports in the schools—they maintain inventories of resources and supports.

BUILD SYSTEMS THAT INTENTIONALLY SUPPORT SUSTAINABILITY

Every aspect in planning and implementation of the CA Framework has been done with purpose and intention that build capacity to achieve sustainability for the initiative. The district branded CA as the initiative that supports the implementation of school-based programs, ensures programs and initiatives are focused on outcomes, engages and aligns programming and funding streams, and utilizes evaluation to focus on efforts to outcomes. Focusing on the results-focused component of partnerships has provided organizational and political sustainability.

Embed Evaluation as Wrap-Around Support to the Initiative

To support the systemic development and implementation of the CA Framework and, hence, the sustainability of the initiative, MNPS has prioritized the integration of evaluation efforts into the framework, structure, and cycle of activities. The CA implementation standards and early identification of shared outcomes and indicators drive the evaluation work.

The district works with an external evaluator to collect, compile, and report evaluative information to the project and to individual schools to (1) monitor and feedback data on indicators of implementation and impact, (2) assess school-level adaptations of the CA framework to identify areas for modification and increased support, and (3) provide tools by which schools can engage networks of results-focused partners, especially through monitoring of disaggregated academic-related data for cohorts of students in programs. Evaluation tools are in place throughout the annual cycle of activities within the CA schools.

Develop a Framework with Process, Output, and Outcome Components

It is not unusual for there to be pressure for funded initiatives to produce immediate results for long-term outcomes. To clarify expectations and focus stakeholders and funders on shorter-term gains, it is important to create a results-based framework that includes indicators of development, implementation, and output that are achievable before the longer-term outcomes may be realized. Creating a framework and timeline that support the capacity to monitor results at all stages, with clearly communicated priorities, processes, and procedures for collecting, managing, analyzing, and reporting data are crucial.

Schools and the CA office monitor implementation through annual self-assessments, periodic school visits, interviews, and artifact reviews. MNPS has a robust data warehouse and a program management module that increases accessibility to whole school and program-specific academic-related data. Examples of implementation indicators include number of and attendance at group partner meetings, and the number of unduplicated students enrolled in programs for academic enrichment, tutoring, character education, and mentoring.

Outcome indicators include data such as average daily attendance, chronic absence, scores on standardized tests, scholarship dollars, discipline incidents, number of parent-teacher conferences, number of accounts and use of the web-based family portal, and results from student, parent, and school staff surveys. Integration of evaluation in the overall development and daily implementation of the framework has proven to be invaluable for the sustainability of our work by adding to the shared understanding of what the initiative is designed to achieve and what the path to outcomes looks like.

Prioritize Site Coordination

Intentional coordination of the community school initiative at the school-level is the fundamental link between systems-level structures, school-level implementation, and services to students, families, and the community. The work done by coordinators to communicate needs and assets at the school-level, collect data on programs, services, and the implementation of the community school strategy informs the ongoing development of systems-level structures and supports. MNPS tried to add the role of "community school coordinator" to various existing school roles in the schools (e.g., school counselor), with less than ideal success.

It is easy to underestimate the time and commitment needed to develop a community school. CA site managers are building community schools while working to change the mind-set of educators around views on equity, poverty, and non-academic factors. CA experienced growth in every aspect of the community school initiative once the local budget funded school-level CA site managers, with 100 percent of time for community school-related work.

Continuously Communicate Shared Expectations to Stakeholders

Community school development and scaling-up involves internal and external partnerships at both the systems and school-levels. The landscape of partnerships is always changing with the introduction and exiting of partnerships, evolving district and city initiatives, changing community needs, and changes in school and district leadership. Since development of the CA initiative began in earnest, MNPS has had two superintendents and almost all of the schools currently developing as CA schools have had multiple executive principals.

Asking providers, organizations, and departments to make changes, be intentional around outcomes, and collaborate with schools and other partners can often be threatening. Clear, constant, and consistent communication and messaging that focuses the initiative around results for students, families, and communities has proven the most successful way to negotiate and nurture these partnerships.

FINAL THOUGHTS

The steadfast and complex nature of problems like poverty, equity, social, emotional, and mental health require comprehensive, yet adaptable solutions. MNPS and its partners built CA to be a collaborative initiative focused on continuous improvement. We must always strive to learn from our mistakes in order to truly serve our students and families effectively.

Challenges and opportunities often represent "two sides of a coin." Community school initiatives are in constant development, and often competition, within a landscape of other prioritized initiatives, political platforms, funding, and advocacy. The challenges that arise within this landscape can represent opportunities for coordination, but require a great deal of patience, diplomacy, transparency, and a desire for being part of a collective.

Funding for a community school initiative or site is an ongoing challenge. Careful assessment of unique and shared resources and needs across schools, coupled with existing and potential funding streams from various sectors provides an opportunity to develop a funding matrix that can serve to develop a collective approach to achieving shared outcomes.

The work of implementing a community school initiative is never complete and needs to exist within a larger system of efforts, joined as a collection of strategies aimed at meeting student and whole school community needs. The district's choice to be the intermediary for CA emphasizes the framework as one that can support other school, district, and community initiatives in a way that aligns the efforts to increase impact on students.

In order for coordinated efforts to succeed, transparent monitoring of structures, processes, and outcomes must be continuous with a willingness to make mid-course corrections. Communication is imperative but also challenging because of the number of individuals and organizations involved and the constant change with all of them. The time needed to plan and implement an initiative or make changes will always take longer than anticipated. Always look ahead at future goals and outcomes, but also remember to celebrate all successes.

REFERENCES

Kania, J., & Kramer, M. (2011, Winter). Collective Impact. *Stanford Social Innovation Review*, (36–41).

Appendix A

Adopted April 2007

STUDENT ENGAGEMENT STANDARDS

The Meaningful Student Engagement Collaborative convened in February and April 2007 to create and adopt these MSE Standards for OUSD implementation. MSE Collaborative members in Spring 2007: All City Council Governing Board, Leadership teachers representing Havenscourt and Castlemont campuses, School Board Director Dobbins, Oakland Youth Commission, Youth Together, Californians for Justice, Asian/Pacific Islander Youth Promoting Advocacy and Leadership, Oakland Kids First!, and OUSD Parent Engagement Specialist.

PRINCIPLES
- Diversity in student leadership (ethnicity, gender, grades, class, sexuality, youth culture, etc) helps to access the influence of many different cliques and groups at schools
- Collaboration between school institutions and community-based groups builds student power and voice
- Student leadership will not take the same form at every school site —sites meet standards through activities that fit with their specific educational philosophy and situation

STANDARDS
Students in leadership class or bodies will demonstrate…

I. Knowledge of self
- Understanding internalized, interpersonal, and institutional oppression and ways to resist
- Knowledge of ethnic studies
- Ability to balance schedule, manage
- Understanding of individual leadership style and situational leadership
- Having personal vision

II. Ability to action plan and lead school improvement projects or campaigns

- Having a vision for educational equity and quality schools
- Knowing how the school runs
- Ability to facilitate meeting
- Understanding models for creating change (service projects, advocacy, organizing, projects and campaigns)
- Ability to work in a team
- Ability to outreach to peers; recruiting, presentations

III. Attitude of ownership of school and education

- Feeling of empowerment and investment in improving school
- Ability to determine one's own future by having an individual and collective vision and plan to reach those visions
- Qualities of persistence
- Ability to access resources and supports when faced with opposition

IV. Understanding of and ability to represent constituents

- Understanding of what it means to be a democratically elected representative
- Ability to get feedback from constituents through different assessments: surveys, interviews, forums
- Commitment to speaking for a group rather than individual (self)
- Ability to create a platform or set of issues from constituents

V. Ability to participate in youth-adult decision making

- Understanding how to participate in youth–adult partnership
- Ability to speak in public
- Ability to write proposals

School Sites will…

Have mechanisms to support student engagement in key school planning decisions

- Student council or other kind of student governing body
- Budget for leadership
- Training for student leaders to participate in action planning, youth-adult partnerships, and governance (via advisory, class, etc.)
- Site based adult support for student leaders
- Students on School Site Council
- Students on Positive Climate Committee
- Student input on other site policies

Participate in district wide student engagement efforts

- Elections for ACC positions
- School board rep elections
- Adult staff participate in ACC activities and professional development
- Students participate in ACC activities

VI. Facilitate student leader access to and relationship with decision makers

- Regular meetings with principal and/or other administrators to dialogue about student concerns
- Training for adult staff on youth-adult partnerships

VII. Facilitate strong student leader relationship to constituents, student body

- Regular elections or other method of broad based selection of student leaders /representatives
- Encouragement and selection of diverse and non-traditional leaders to participate in leadership
- Mechanisms for on-going dialogue and feedback around issues: student senate, surveys, forums, assemblies, etc.
- Provide opportunities for every child to participate in leadership in some way

The District will…
___

Support district wide student engagement body

- Convene student leaders, formal and informal, selected from a broad based process to discuss student issues as well as plan projects or campaigns for school improvement
- Provide for ACC budget
- Support youth-adult decision making at district level
- Create office of student engagement
- Provide adult support (staffing) of district wide work
- Facilitate regular meetings between ACC students and district level decision makers including school board members, superintendent
- Adopt Student Bill of Rights

Involve students in district level policy making

- Include youth voice in district wide data and assessment tools, provide feedback to students as well as adults
- Draw from district wide student leadership body to sit on various policy making committees as appropriate

Involve a broad and diverse group of students in district wide engagement body

- Ensure marginalized student voices are included and heard in district wide student engagement body (ie: LGTBQ youth, immigrant and ESL students, refugee students, foster youth, etc…)
- Create mechanisms to involve every student in leadership in some way

Support Adults to lead processes and participate in youth–adult decision-making

- Provide training for adults on sharing decision making with youth to adults working at the District
- Provide training for adults on sharing decision making with youth for adults at the school

Support Student School Board Representatives

- Provide training for Student School Board Representatives
- Broad based selection process for Student School Board Representatives
- Facilitate mechanism for on-going feedback between Student School Board Representatives and constituents

Support site based student engagement efforts

- Encourage sites to meet student engagement standards
- Provide professional development for site staff to support student engagement
- Provide adult support at the district level (staffing) to coordinate work across sites, support site level staff
- Provide age appropriate activities and curriculum for sites to use
- Plan training for students on site based decision-making bodies (such as School Site Council)

Appendix B

Oakland Student Bill of Rights and Responsibilities

All students in the Oakland Unified School District have the right to:

1) Clear Academic and Social Standards
A clear statement of the academic and social standards that
   a. Define what students are expected to learn at every grade level and
   b. Define what code of conduct is expected from students and adults
   c. Define the support students and families can expect from the educational system
   (so that students can meet the standards).

2) Textbooks and Materials for Class
Proper learning materials, (lab) equipment, and resources they need to succeed in their classes.

3) Clean and Safe Facilities
Under state law, students have the right to safe and clean facilities.

4) Diverse and Effective Teachers and Counselors
This means the adults that support us are able to relate to students, are able to adapt their teaching methods, are prepared, have experience, and are always available when students need them.

5) "AG" Courses – College and Career for All
A course of instruction that will enable all students to compete for admission to any public university in the state, have living wage jobs and careers, and participate as an active community member upon graduating from high school.
College and career recruitment must be as visible, or more visible, than military recruitment on our campuses.

6) Safe and Caring Schools
A safe and supportive school environment has teachers, counselors, student support staff, cafeteria staff, school security officers and administrators that truly care about students. A safe school is created when we have:
   a) Code of Conduct*,
   b) Wrap Around Student Support, and
   c) Restorative Justice programs and discipline systems that help students to engage in their education rather than punish them or push them out of school.
*Student leaders help create the Code of Conduct, that both students and staff are held accountable to

7) Fair Testing

Schools should provide fair and diverse assessments that are used to measure how well students understand the material. Tests should be used by teachers to improve their teaching methods. Classroom curriculum and assessment must be connected.

8) Cultural Pride and Dignity

Students have the right to positively affirm and learn more about their culture:

a. Ethnic Studies courses on ethnic history and culture are available at each high school campus

b. Monolingual and Bilingual students can be certified in their language. This means they are able to prove mastery of their own (foreign) language, and mastery in other subjects (math, science,) in their language, so that most of their instruction time can be dedicated to learning English.

c. All students have the right to keep, develop, display, and celebrate their cultures publicly through language, art, and student activities.

9) Decision Making

School culture and practices that allow students and families have a say in school decisions, including representation on the school site councils, the hiring of staff, and in the District/ statewide education policy.

10) Student Support Services Report Card

Student and family friendly report card measuring how well the school is providing student support services, and meeting students' rights listed herein.

(Last Modified on March 1, 2012)

Notes

FOREWORD

1. Jeannie Oakes is Presidential Professor of Education Equity Emeritus, UCLA, and Senior Fellow in Residence, Learning Policy Institute.

2. The report can be found online at https://learningpolicyinstitute.org/product /community-schools-effectiveschool-improvement-report.

INTRODUCTION

1. To view the standards, visit www.communityschools.org/standards.

CHAPTER ONE: THE COMMUNITY SCHOOLS MOVEMENT

1. The concept of what constitutes a "movement" is worthy of discussion. For the purposes of this chapter, I refer to a "community school movement" that is characterized by networks of organizations and individuals that identify as community school advocates and who are working together to advance the strategy.

2. In this chapter I use "traditional school" to describe schools that are not community schools.

3. For examples of local policies visit http://www.communityschools.org /policy_advocacy/local.aspx.

CHAPTER TWO: THE IMAGINEERS OF
COMMUNITY SCHOOL LEADERSHIP

1. Imagineers are the group Walt Disney named to engage in creative projects that combine their artistic and engineering skills. The principals and other leaders in schools embody the legacy of the imagineering spirit as they put together ideas, people, and resources to create, implement, and sustain community schools. https://disneyimaginations.com/about-imaginations/about-imagineering/.

2. The principles that undergird the implementation of community schools appear in a national report from three organizations: the Institute for Educational Leadership (and home of the Coalition of Community Schools), the Center for Popular Democracy, which is partnering with the National Education Association, to foster development of community schools in more locations, and the Southern Education Fund collaborated on a key report that tells the story and highlights the major principles and practices necessary for a community school. https://populardemocracy.org/news/publications/community-schools -transforming-struggling-schools-thriving-schools. Other national organizations and efforts, including the Black Lives Matter education agenda, have named community schools as a positive and promising reform effort.

3. A closing circle is an ancient and indigenous ritual in which all members of the community have an opportunity and a responsibility to contribute to collective knowledge and wisdom.

4. The Community Learning Exchange (CLE) "hows" are protocols on the Institute for Educational Leadership website: http://iel.org/protocols.

5. The Coalition of Community Schools—over 20 years old—is housed at the Institute for Educational Leadership in Washington, D.C. It holds a bi-yearly national forum to highlight the work of community schools and includes schools and their districts in its network.

6. Lucy Calkins is a professor at Columbia University Teachers College. Her approach to reading and writing has been an influence on many schools, districts, and teachers nationally and internationally. http://readingandwritingproject.org/.

7. Abstract resources are those school resources—like time and relationships—that have to be cocreated. The school may need monetary resources to actually engage in the deepening relational trust and re-imagining use of time, but without the foundations of abstract resources (strong climate and culture), often we use the money resources for professional learning that does not have any effect (Grubb, 2009).

8. Caring Schools Curriculum is a nationally recognized program to address students' social emotional outcomes. https://www.collaborativeclassroom.org /caring-school-community.

9. The original funding in the elementary school came from QEIA (Quality Education Investment Act) money from the state; in addition, the district budgeting process now recognizes the need for the transition time and the funding necessary to do that. At the K–8, a donation by Sales Force to the school district is the current funding, but, in any case, he expects to ensure that the necessary funding is available as the results from the linked day approach are important for students and families as well as the staff understanding.

10. The district has had multiple leadership changes; however, the district is still committed to be and become a full-service community school district. The school won the district's first Community Schools Award and was selected to host a conference on community schools in the 2016–2017 school year. The school, with support of consultants, designed a blueprint for how they want to move forward in 2017–2018. http://www.ousd.org/domain/4019.

11. The Community School Manager (CSM) coordinates the attendance team and sits on the school leadership team, which meets every week and alternates focus on instruction and on school culture and climate.

12. Like Principal One, the use of 1:1 diagnostic and reading progress using the Fountas and Pinnell reading tests, which are time-consuming, but helpful to teachers in moving toward personalized learning for each student. The F&P offer ways to track reading levels and make appropriate changes in grouping and additional supports.

13. Many school educators use data that are a mismatch with their intent. That is, the psychometric intent of assessments does not always match the use (see Militello, Sireci, & Schweid, 2008; Militello & Heffernan, 2009). School leaders are uniquely situated to provide teachers with data that can inform their practice.

CHAPTER THREE: COMMUNITY SCHOOL TEACHER LEADERS ENHANCE LEARNING

1. Data retrieved from https://data1.cde.ca.gov/dataquest/.

2. Data retrieved from National Center for Education Statistics. https://nces .ed.gov/fastfacts/display.asp?id=51.

3. Data retrieved from https://data1.cde.ca.gov/dataquest/.

CHAPTER FIVE: THE COMMUNITY
SCHOOL COORDINATOR

1. Children's Aid, formerly the Children's Aid Society, has been operating community schools since 1992. Drawing from its expertise as a lead agency partner, Children's Aid National Center for Community Schools (NCCS) builds capacity; guides practice; disseminates knowledge; and advocates for policies at the city, state, and national levels.

2. The School Leadership Team is a governing body that determines every NYC school's overall educational vision, its goals and priorities, the strategies that will be used to achieve that vision and the alignment of resources to accomplish those strategies.

3. See http://www.communityschools.org/standards/.

CHAPTER SIX: TRANSFORMATIVE
FAMILY ENGAGEMENT IN
COMMUNITY SCHOOLS

1. We use the terms "parents" and "families" interchangeably in this chapter, to acknowledge that the adults in the parenting role are often grandparents, aunts and uncles, or other caregivers; regardless, the same principles of engagement apply.

2. See http://www.communityschools.org/standards/.

3. To understand what the deficit mentality is, read Weiner, L. (2006). Challenging deficit thinking. *Educational Leadership, 64*(1), 42–45.

4. There is extensive research on the impact of implicit and overt bias among teachers and school staff, see Gershenson, Holt, & Papageorge, 2015; Gershenson & Papageorge, 2017; Goff, Jackson, Di Leone, Culotta, & Ditomasso, 2014; Parker, 2015.

5. Regarding racial diversity among school staff, read U.S. Department of Education. (2016). *The state of racial diversity in the educator workforce.* Retrieved from https://www2.ed.gov/rschstat/eval/highered/racial-diversity/state-racial-diversity-workforce.pdf.

6. More examples of effective parent engagement strategies in community schools can be found in: Center for Popular Democracy and the NYC Coalition for Educational Justice. (n.d.). *Community schools toolkit.* Retrieved from http://populardemocracy.org/sites/default/files/Community-Schools-Toolkit.pdf.

7. This framework was developed by Dr. Karen Mapp and adopted by the U.S. Department of Education. A paper on the framework can be found here:

http://www.sedl.org/pubs/framework/FE-Cap-Building.pdf and examples of the framework in action can be found here: https://www2.ed.gov/documents/family -community/frameworks-resources.pdf.

8. The Parent-Teacher Home Visit Project has many resources to support this practice: www.pthvp.org.

9. To learn more about Parent-Teacher Home Visits, go to: www.pthvp.org.

10. To learn more about Academic Parent-Teacher Teams, go to: https://www .wested.org/service/academic-parent-teacher-teams-family-engagement/.

11. To learn more about the Parent Mentor Program, go to: http://www.lsna .net/Issues-and-programs/Schools-and-Youth/Parent-Mentor-Program.html.

12. For more information about Abriendo Puertas, go to: http://ap-od.org/.

13. For the Parent Training Curriculum Modules visit https://drive.google .com/drive/u/0/folders/1WfvioX3K_Nbcj4Yaeg32KumByRItYT7r.

CHAPTER SEVEN: VOICES FOR EQUITY

1. We would like to thank the many individuals of Oakland who have contributed their insight and time to inform the writing of this chapter. Any shortcomings or discrepancies in the chapter are our own responsibility. We would also like to acknowledge Raquel Jimenez, for her foundational work and continued leadership in student and family engagement as a core equity strategy, and the many educators, adult allies, and partner organizations in Oakland who have stepped back and stepped up to make room for young people. And most of all, we would like to thank the thousands of youth who have and who will continue to contribute their heart, souls, and time in the service of our community. Oakland is a better place for their actions, and this story would not exist without them.

2. Physical and emotional safety, supportive relationships, opportunities to belong, opportunities for skill building, support for efficacy and mattering, positive social norms, appropriate structures, and integration of family, school, and community efforts are all attributes of positive youth development settings (Eccles & Gootman 2002).

3. Proposition 187 was later ruled unconstitutional by a district federal court. In 1999, then-governor Gray Davis halted state appeals of this ruling.

4. These groups included a multitude of organizations such as Kids First, Youth Together, Movement Strategy Center, Ella Baker Center, Third Eye Movement, Critical Resistance, and School of Unity and Liberation (SOUL), among others, many of which are still active at the time of this writing.

5. Compared to a white child born in the affluent Oakland Hills neighborhood, an African American child born in West Oakland is seven times more likely to

be born into poverty, four times less likely to read at grade level by grade 4, and 5.6 times more likely to drop out of school (Alameda County Public Health Department, 2008).

6. The Student Power Resolution articulated a district policy that would: (1) broaden the scope of action of student councils (to include issues like school safety, discipline, teacher quality, and curriculum); (2) increase funds, facilities, and support so that student councils could turn their ideas into actions and policies; (3) ensure that elected student leaders could and would negotiate and represent student concerns to school-based administrators; (4) provide open forums where students could bring up concerns, problems, and ideas for school improvement; and (5) increase the number of leadership classes so that more students could move into leadership positions (Goldwasser 2004; Kids First Oakland, 2017).

7. The Student Power Resolution was developed by a coalition of youth organizations, and drew from a large-scale youth-led participant action research project. Youth surveyed 1,000 of their peers at three high schools and held multiple forums to understand the root causes of high school dropout. Youth organizers analyzed survey data, carefully reviewed student comments, and held a series of student forums to engage a broader student audience in the analysis of the data and the development of policy recommendations. The Student Power Resolution reflects findings from that research. For a thorough case study of the youth organizing during this time, see Kirshner 2015.

8. The Meaningful Student Engagement Collaborative convened in February and April 2007 to create and adopt these MSE Standards for OUSD implementation. MSE collaborative members in Spring 2007 included: All City Council Governing Board, Leadership teachers representing Havenscourt and Castlemont campuses, School Board Director Dobbins, Oakland Youth Commission, Youth Together, Californians for Justice, Asian/Pacific Islander Youth Promoting Advocacy and Leadership, Oakland Kids First!, and OUSD Parent Engagement Specialist.

9. The first staff person hired was an OUSD alumna and current youth organizer who had been deeply involved in developing the MSE Standards and advocating for educational reform.

10. A review of the current MSE Standards will show a new cover page, like the other task force generated documents, along with a new date.

11. Although most district schools offer at least some of the programmatic elements described above, to be a designated district community school, a site has a community school manager (CSM): a funded position that manages and integrates the additional functions of the community school and plays a primary role implementing the organizational strategies. CSMs identify gaps in programs and services, manage and maintain quality partnerships, ensure that student/family supports are well-coordinated and integrated (often leading cross-disciplinary teams), and facilitate youth, family, and staff engagement.

12. The first cohort of community schools included high schools with established school-based health centers or sites located in high-poverty communities with strong existing partnership. Prior to the district-wide initiative, some OUSD schools operated as community schools through other initiatives such as Atlantic Philanthropies and Elev8. Subsequently, two additional cohorts have been established through an application process, prioritizing schools in high-need communities.

13. Since that initial merger, the Department of Community Schools and Student Services has inherited some additional pieces, including a segment of early learning.

14. For more on OUSD community schools, see Fehrer, K., and Leos-Urbel, J. (2015). *Oakland Unified School District Community Schools: Understanding Implementation Efforts to Support Students, Teachers, and Families.* Stanford, CA: John W. Gardner Center for Youth and Their Communities. Or Fehrer, K., Leos-Urbel, J. "We're One Team": Examining Community School Implementation Strategies in Oakland. *Educ. Sci.* 2016, *6*, 26.

15. An adult ally is an individual who wholeheartedly believes in the potential of young people to contribute their strengths and skills for the benefit of themselves and their communities. They are often supportive mentors who encourage participation, positive development, and organization in their students. They also listen, learn, and appreciate young people's assets.

16. To do this, the OSFCE offers an array of programming to bolster student engagement, including MSE Leadership Teacher Community of Practice (a professional learning community and coaching support for teachers and adult allies); the ACCSU Governing Board and Youth Voice with School Culture (monthly meetings of the ACCSU to involve a wider base of student representatives from high schools across the district); Middle School Peer Resource Conference and High School Youth Action Summit (a series of events to support student engagement in issues such as school health, academic readiness, school culture and climate, and more); and Youth Voice with Continuous Improvement (an initiative tied to supporting middle and high school student participation on school site councils and the district-wide LCAP Student Advisory). Each of these programs represent structured and institutionalized opportunities for young people to be supported as leaders and agents of change.

17. See http://www.communityschools.org/standards/.

18. The contract also includes a commitment to keep a minimum of 2.0 GPA (if they drop below that, they have a semester to get their grades up) and attend 90 percent of the meetings.

19. The Local Control and Accountability Plan (LCAP) is the site-level plan associated with California's new Local Control Funding Formula (LCFF), which provides schools with greater flexibility on determining spending priorities and awards additional funds to schools with high-need populations. The three-year plan that describes the goals, actions, services, and expenditures to

support positive student outcomes that address state and local priorities. The LCAP provides an opportunity for local educational agencies to share their stories of how, what, and why programs and services are selected to meet their local needs. For more on LCAP and LCFF, see https://www.cde.ca.gov/re/lc/.

20. In the 2015–2016 school year, All City Council Student Union delegates and LCAP Student Advisory collaborated in a year-long youth action research project on the LCAP goals that they identified to be the most connected to students. The research resulted in recommendations on increasing student voice in staff hiring, creating a more responsive facility maintenance system, and improving accessibility of the district's credit recovery system. Students identified the following LCAP goals as most connected with student experience: Goal 1—Graduates are College and Career Ready; Goal 2—Students are Proficient in State Academic Standards; Goal 5—Students are Engaged in School Everyday; along with their own added focus/goal area, "Basic Services."

21. For example, that OUSD's current counselor to student ratio is approximately 1:500 while the national recommendation is 1:250, 65 percent of students currently doing credit recovery do not know their A-G status, and 24.6 percent of ninth graders and 31.9 percent of tenth graders did not meet the credit requirements to complete that grade level.

22. The distinctions between "informing" and "consulting" youth versus adult/youth equity are made clear in the Ladder of Youth Voice, included in figure 7.2, and frequently referenced by students and adults in the developing of this chapter.

CHAPTER EIGHT: COMMUNITY SCHOOL PARTNERSHIPS AND CONTINUOUS IMPROVEMENT

1. See http://www.communityschools.org/standards/.

CHAPTER NINE: THE ROLE OF THE SCHOOL DISTRICT

1. Career Academies utilize a small learning community approach, career-themed curricula, and partnerships supported by an advisory board. For more, visit the National Career Academy Coalition at https://www.ncacinc.com/.

About the Editors

JoAnne Ferrara is associate dean of undergraduate programs and a professor. Prior to joining the Manhattanville faculty, she held positions as a general and special education teacher, a literacy coach, and school administrator for the New York City Department of Education. JoAnne is an experienced educator specializing in community schools and university partnerships. She is the series co-editor for Professional Development School Research Book Series, and the section coeditor of PDS Partners. JoAnne is the recipient of the American Educational Research Association's Claudia A. Balach PDS SIG Research Award and the Jason Kinsey-Friend of the National Association of Professional Development School's Award. These awards are granted to individuals that demonstrate an ongoing ownership in P–12 and university collaborators research, investigation of issues that impact student outcomes or teacher professional development, an ongoing interest in teachers as researchers, and a sustained program of research and inquiry. In addition to her campus duties, she is the professional development school (PDS) network coordinator and the college liaison to the Thomas A. Edison professional development school in Port Chester, New York, a partnership she created in 2002.

Reuben Jacobson is director of the Education Policy and Leadership Program at the American University in Washington, D.C. Previously, Reuben served as the deputy director for the Coalition for Community Schools at the Institute for Educational Leadership (IEL). Reuben has been a leader in the community schools field for 10 years, helping to grow and strengthen community schools by working with national partners and local leaders.

He has written widely about school and community partnerships. Prior to joining IEL Reuben worked at the American Institutes for Research in Washington, D.C., as a research analyst in education. In addition, he spent two challenging and wonderful years teaching fifth and sixth grade students in D.C. Public Schools as a D.C. Teaching Fellow. He is an alumnus of IEL's Education Policy Fellowship Program and the Education Pioneers Fellowship. Reuben has a BA from the University of Wisconsin, a master's degree in education policy from the George Washington University, a Master of Arts in Teaching degree from American University, and a PhD in education policy from the University of Maryland–College Park.

About the Contributors

Natasha Capers is the coordinator and parent leader of the New York City Coalition of Educational Justice (CEJ), an organization that seeks to end the inequities in New York City public schools. A Brooklyn native, she attended public schools all her life and her goal now is to give parents the tools to use their power and wisdom to dismantle a system that underserves them and their children.

Carl Egner is program coordinator for the Community Schools Initiative (CSI) of the Chicago Public Schools since 2012. Before that, he spent over 20 years working on various community development projects in the United States and abroad, and then spent some years in academia during which he earned a master's degree in education policy. He is happy to be back again working more in direct contact with the grassroots level, and being able to work on his belief that schools can and should be a central focus for community development.

Kendra Fehrer, PhD, is research associate at the John W. Gardner Center for Youth and Their Communities at Stanford University. Trained in anthropology and community development, she brings a culturally informed and community-oriented perspective to her work. Since 2014, she has been working with Oakland Unified School District in a research partnership aimed to support OUSD community school implementation.

Diane W. Gómez, PhD, is associate professor and chairperson of the Educational Leadership and Special Subjects Department in the School of Education at Manhattanville College. She has served as professional development school liaison in two full-service community schools of the Manhattanville Changing Suburbs' districts. Before becoming a faculty member and administrator in higher education, she was a high school Spanish and ESL teacher in public, parochial, and special education residential treatment schools in New York State and New York City. She has written several articles related to professional development schools, dual language programs, and English learners. Her most recent book publications are: *Challenges Facing Suburban Schools: Promising Responses to Changing Student Populations* (Rowman & Littlefield Education, 2017) and *Literacy Leadership in Changing Schools: Ten Keys for Successful Professional Development* (2016); and chapters in three of the five volumes of the Breaking the Mold series (Rowman & Littlefield, 2010, 2012, 2014) and in *Creating Visions for University/School Partnerships: A Volume in Professional Development School Research* (2014).

Lissette Gomez, LCSW (licensed clinical social worker), is director of special projects with the Children's Aid National Center for Community Schools. Lissette has served in the fields of nonprofit management, after-school education, and community schools as a leader, manager, advocate, staff developer, and consultant. Prior to joining NCCS, Lissette served as vice president of Development Without Limits (DWL), a private consulting firm, where she provided overall strategic leadership and vision for the organization's NYC-based operations with over 20 years of experience, Lissette has focused expertise in professional development, coaching, curriculum development, program development, and management. In September 2011, Lissette was one of 22 Latinas across the country to successfully complete the National Hispana Leadership Institute (NHLI).

Megan Hester has worked in the education justice movement for two decades as an organizer, trainer, and researcher. She is currently director of the Education Justice Research and Organizing Collaborative at the NYU Metro Center, where she provides research, policy, and strategic support to education organizing groups in New York City and nationally.

Sarah Hurst has 20 years' experience as a fund-raising consultant, with expertise in preK–12 and postsecondary education. She assists clients in grant writing, research, program design, evaluation, budgeting, strategic planning, and publications. Sarah has a BA from Saint Louis University and an MBA from the UCLA Anderson School of Management.

Aurora Lopez, MPH, is the meaningful Student Engagement Liaison for the Oakland United School District. In this role, she trains students and educators to become copartners in decision making and has spearheaded efforts for student-lead policies and practices for educational equity. Her trajectory spans over a decade of service in community organizing, youth development, and policy advocacy.

Deborah Lowe is principal of the Humanitas Academy of Art and Technology, an LAUSD pilot high school founded by LAUSD teachers in 2010 on the Esteban E. Torres Campus. She began her English teaching career at Roosevelt High School in Boyle Heights in 1999 and was a founding teacher of the school she now leads. She is a nationally board-certified teacher with an undergraduate degree from Brown University and a master's degree in education from UCLA. She has taught in the UCLA Teacher Education Program, worked extensively at the UCLA Writing Project, and presented her work at national and state conferences. Under Ms. Lowe's leadership, the Humanitas Academy of Art and Technology was described in its accreditation review as "an innovative school . . . that models the best practices of 21st century teaching and learning."

Tony Majors, PhD, is a career educator having spent his 23-year career serving as a teacher, coach, principal, and now executive officer for Metropolitan Nashville Public Schools. Dr. Majors manages 14 divisions of the Metro Nashville Public School System, and his responsibilities range from social and emotional learning, wraparound services, student health, and community engagement. As a principal, Dr. Majors was awarded the National Community School of Excellence Award, a GRAMMY Foundation award, and Principal of the Year. His national work includes the PASSAGE initiative that focuses on discipline disparities, CASEL which emphasizes the social and emotional development of students, and Community Achieves which is Nashville's brand for the development of full service community schools.

Alison McArthur, EdS, is coordinator for Community Achieves; the MNPS-led community school initiative. Alison taught at Glencliff High School, a 2011 Coalition Awards for Excellence winner, for 13 years. She also served in the academy coach role as Metro Nashville Public Schools began the redesign of high schools into small learning communities.

Matthew Militello, PhD (Michigan State University), is the Wells Fargo Distinguished Professor in Educational Leadership at East Carolina University. He has held faculty positions at North Carolina State University and the University of Massachusetts at Amherst. Prior to his academic career, Militello was a middle and high public school teacher, assistant principal, and principal in Michigan. Militello has more than 75 publications including co-authoring six books. He can be reached at militellom14@ecu.edu.

Kelly Noser, PhD, has consulted with MNPS for over 10 years, utilizing evaluation tools to deepen and individualize the development of district-led, multi-school initiatives, most notably the Academies of Nashville and Community Achieves. Noser will continue to work with the district and schools to focus on monitoring implementation and impact indicators, within a continuous improvement approach to developing MNPS's community school initiative.

Ellen Pais is a strategic planning consultant and executive coach. She is the former president and CEO of Los Angeles Education Partnership. She has 30 years of experience in community building, community relations, and the law. Ellen led the process to consolidate LAEP's work into a comprehensive, holistic model for school transformation defined by the organization's Six Core Elements for school reform. She was the driving force behind LAEP's expansion and development of community collaboratives and community-school partnerships and is a past member of the steering committee of the National Coalition for Community Schools. Prior to LAEP, she was CEO for Planned Parenthood of Pasadena, co-founder and chair of Community Coalition for Quality Public Schools, and a lawyer at Orrick, Herrington & Sutcliffe LLP and the Los Angeles City Attorney's Office. She earned a JD from American University, Washington College of Law, and a BA from UC Berkeley.

Adeline Ray is senior manager for the Chicago Public Schools (CPS) Community Schools Initiative (CSI). Having transformed over 200 schools into vibrant centers of their communities, she oversees all aspects of the initiative for CPS including grant development and reporting, strategic implementation, evaluation design, and data sharing. Ms. Ray was honored in 2016 with the Coalition for Community Schools' Community Schools Initiative Leadership Award. She serves on the Illinois State Board of Education's 21st CCLC Professional Development Advisory Group, ACT Now Leadership and Community School Committees, and cochairs the Coalition's Community Schools Leadership Network.

Jennie Carey Rosenbaum joined LAEP in 2009 and served as community-school coordinator for six and a half years. She has been in the field of education, youth development, leadership, and community development for more than 17 years as a tutor, teacher, and volunteer to nonprofits focused on youth development, leadership, and social entrepreneurship; immigrant parent engagement; empowering young Latino males; college access; and community schools. She has a BA from the College of William and Mary and an EdM from Harvard's Graduate School of Education. She currently works for the EduCare Foundation on social-emotional learning and college access at the Social Justice Humanitas Academy as the ACE Initiative site administrator.

Liz Thacker works in Knoxville, Tennessee, for Great Schools Partnership leading the Northwest Middle Community School. She has been a coordinator for six years starting both an elementary and middle community school. Liz serves as the cochair for the Coordinators Network.

Lynda Tredway is senior associate for the Leaders for Today and Tomorrow Project, a catalyst for engaging IHEs, school districts, nonprofits in uncovering and coordinating their efforts in social justice preparation and support of urban and rural leaders in our most vulnerable schools. As founding coordinator of the Principal Leadership Institute (PLI) at UC Berkeley's Graduate School of Education (2000–2012), she designed and taught in the program and provided professional development to principals and assistant principals in urban districts. Her recent publications include "Actions Matter: How School Leaders Enact Equity Principles" in the *Handbook of*

Urban School Leadership, coauthored with Jessica Rigby; and *Leading from the Inside Out: Expanding Roles of Teachers in Equitable Schools*, coauthored with W. Norton Grubb. She is currently the program coordinator for the East Carolina University EdD program in Southeast Asia and supports 15 doctoral candidates and teaches in the program.

Jessica Wadle is currently assistant principal of the Humanitas Academy of Art and Technology, an LAUSD pilot high school, which she co-founded in 2010. Jessica entered teaching through the Teach For America program in 1993 at Roosevelt High School in Boyle Heights, Los Angeles. She was an English teacher and a literacy coach at Roosevelt for 17 years. In 1999 Jessica earned her National Board Certification in Adolescent/Young Adult English Language Arts. Upon earning certification, Jessica worked as a coach for other LAUSD teachers seeking National Board Certification. Starting in 2002, Jessica also served as a literacy coach for low-performing, urban middle schools through the Los Angeles Education Partnership. In her current role as assistant principal at the Humanitas Academy of Art and Technology, Jessica works closely with teachers to support the school-wide instructional program.